© 2023 Cindy Georgakas

Re-Create & Celebrate

All rights reserved. No part of this publication may be reproduced, stored in a retrieval system or transmitted in any form or by any means, electronic, mechanical, photocopying, recording or otherwise without the prior permission of the publisher or the author of the relevant work who retains the copyright of his work in accordance with the provisions of the Copyright, Designs and Patents Act 1988 or under the terms of any license permitting limited copying issued by the Copyright Licensing Agency.

ISBN: 978-1-7394044-1-3

Published by Experiments in Fiction
www.experimentsinfiction.com

Cindy Georgakas

RE-CREATE & CELEBRATE

7 Steps to turn your Dreams into Reality

A Teaching Memoir and Workbook

Re-Create & Celebrate

7 STEPS TO TURN YOUR DREAMS INTO REALITY

CINDY GEORGAKAS

I DEDICATE THIS BOOK TO YOU MY HUMBLE READER. IT IS MY BIGGEST HOPE THAT YOU MAY FIND THE SEEDS OF YOUR STRENGTH AND COURAGE TO TURN YOUR DREAMS INTO REALITY, CELEBRATING YOUR AUTHENTIC SELF AND LOVING YOURSELF THROUGH EVERY STEP OF THE JOURNEY.

DESIRE + COMMITMENT = RESULTS

— CINDY GEORGAKAS

About the Author

Cindy studied Therapeutic Recreation at San Jose State University, California, where she worked in convalescent hospitals and wellness centers and got certified in group exercise and personal training. She later managed Golden Venus Health Spa in San Francisco and went on to teach classes all down the Peninsula, opening her own Aerobic studio in San Mateo, California at the same time as Jane Fonda opened her studio in San Francisco. Cindy has taught and trained 15 instructors. She has been a life coach since 1979, and is certified by Dr. Chérie Carter Scott, the renowned "Mother of Life Coaching" and New York Times bestselling author. In her own practice, Cindy developed the program, "12 Stars to a Slimmer You" and the workshop "Putting your Dreams into Action."

When the pandemic hit, Cindy continued writing her monthly newsletter for clients, and then started blogging more regularly to keep them motivated while she taught online classes. She also began writing poetry, and was invited to be a monthly contributing author for MasticadoresUSA, an online literary magazine. She has been published by Spillwords Press, where she was voted Author of the Month in May 2023. Her work has appeared in three Anthologies: *Utmost Feelings* Compiled by Ashta Srivastava (True Dreamster, 2021), *Wounds I Healed* (Experiments in Fiction, 2022) and *Hidden in Childhood* (Literary Revelations, 2023).

Praise for *Re-Create & Celebrate*

"It is not always easy to trust ourselves, to venture out of our comfort zones, and go for our dreams, however, Cindy Georgakas has successfully done this in an eloquent way."
—Dr. Chérie Carter-Scott, New York Times Bestselling Author of *If Life is a Game, These are the Rules*

"This book is a powerful asset during psychotherapy, especially for clients who ask for work between sessions. Cindy's creative use of humor and poetry show the depth of her wisdom."— Bonnie Sabrina McGuire, Psychoanalyst & LMFT (retired)

"As a memoir, the book is a testament to the power of positivity in our lives. There is resilience, hope, and healing." — Gabriela Marie Milton, Author, Editor, Publisher

"An inspiring book of anecdotes and ideas for personal exploration and growth. Positive, uplifting, and wholly possible. Highly recommended." — D. Wallace Peach, Bestselling Author of *Catling's Bane*

"This book offers readers tools to converse with their authentic selves with grace and ease." — Barbara Harris Leonhard, Author, *Three-Penny memories: A Poetic Memoir*

"*Re-Create & Celebrate* is a book that leaves the reader inspired. Georgakas' decades of experience is poured out in each chapter." — Yvette Prior, PhD, Work Psychologist & University Professor

"Cindy's well-crafted writing takes you on a journey… using her personal experiences to teach readers how to live life to its fullest". — Pooja Gudka, Website Owner & Entrepreneur

"This book is a must-have for helping readers refocus on their overall health and wellness." — Kym Gordon Moore, MBA, Author of *We Are Poetry: Lessons I Didn't Learn in a Textbook*

"The author has allowed herself to be so very vulnerable with us in this little volume, in a compassionate, loving effort to help other human beings live their very best lives."
— David Bogomolny, Writer, The Jewish Agency for Israel

"This book is insightful with the potential to change people's lives. I highly recommend it if you are ready to move forward in your life."
— Grace Y. Estevez -Reddy, Poet

"Cindy takes us on an inner journey of discovery. This book will open your eyes to new possibilities in your life."
— Dwight L. Roth, Poet

Contents

Preface
by Dr Chérie Carter-Scott — 13
Introduction — 15
Step 1: Finding the True You — 24
Step 2: Finding Your Purpose — 42
Step 3: Finding Your Want and Why — 61
Step 4: Plan of Action— Reaching Your Goals — 76
Step 5: Loving Yourself — 90
Step 6: Processing Feelings — 100
Step 7: Falling off the Wagon, Burnout & Support — 111
Afterward: Celebrate! — 148
Acknowledgements — 150

Preface
by Dr Chérie Carter-Scott

Cindy was one of my first participants when I started my business, Motivational Management Service (MMS). She was young and eager to learn. She had an active mind and second-guessed everything, and yet she was open and willing to discuss her sensitivities and abandonment issues in the first workshop I created called the S.E.W. (Self Esteem Workshop) which is now called The Inter-negotiation Workshop.

Her attention to detail, insight, and ability to connect with other participants were some of her greatest assets. She co-led sessions, and I witnessed her growth as she began to see clients privately, having taken the coach's training. Her ability to bring this practice into her own work as a fitness coach, massage therapist, trainer and manager was inspiring, and the way she moved into teaching so many modalities while working full-time was astounding to me.

I'm in awe of her mothering ability, and the close dynamic that she shares with her children, while she continues to be there for clients, family and friends.

Cindy is a true illustration of the success which can be achieved by attending my coaching sessions. She continues to expand into what she is called to do at every stage of life, and stops at nothing, as evidenced by her ability to put her heart and soul into her writing, sharing her coaching experience and wisdom with the world, to help others uncover their hidden gifts and be the best version of themselves.

Chérie Carter-Scott, Ph.D., MCC
Bestselling author of *If Life is a Game, These are the Rules: 10 Rules for Being Human*

Introduction

Do you wake up in the morning, full of joy and zest, or do you want to throw the covers over your head and hide? Are you living your life, your way, or are you following in someone else's shadow? Life is meant to be lived in accordance with our inner callings, with what is true for us. Life is meant to be celebrated every day.

There will always be moments when we wake up on the wrong side of the bed, spill our coffee, get sick, etc., but if you are constantly in a state of doom and gloom, and have lost your zest for living, it's time to take a long hard look at what you want. Do you wake up with gratitude in your heart, eager to start the day? Or do you dread waking up, as you are full of anxiety and fear?

Perhaps you were living the life you envisioned, before a shattering life event changed everything unexpectedly, causing you to fall apart and find yourself stricken with grief or pain. The top stressors in life are: the death of a loved one; divorce; moving; major illness and job loss. Any and all of these things can stop you in your tracks immediately. It's important to be gentle with yourself when you experience such changes, and get the support you need from family, friends, and professionals. This will help you through the difficult time of transition, so you can bounce back with resilience and find joy again.

We all have times in our life where we are stricken by grief, sorrow or rage that brings us to our knees and leaves us paralyzed. Having a strong support network is critical, as this enables us to remember who we were before the tragedy occurred. Sometimes, we must dig into our past to clear out the debris of childhood trauma that this event might have triggered, allowing us to heal. In much the same way, a doctor undertakes surgery on a damaged body part. Until we get to the root cause, old wounds can continue to fester, become internalized, and never heal, so it's important we don't try to sweep these painful episodes from our past under the carpet.

Too often, we become trapped by the idea of what we think other people want for us, and we don't stop to check in with ourselves to see if we are being authentic and true to our life purpose. We end up on autopilot, living a life someone else has chosen for us.

If you are sick and tired of being sick and tired, and are ready to live the life you always dreamed of, then this book is here to guide you. I'm delighted to share my life experience and secrets with you, in the hope that you, too, can turn your dreams into reality. I know it's possible: do you? You may be a little skeptical, and perhaps you think it's not possible because you have tried so many things before, and they did not work out. I didn't think it was possible in my life either at a certain point, and I'm now living life in panoramic color, exactly the way I want, and enjoying every moment to its fullest. Let me tell you a little secret: I know it's also possible for you to live the life you have always envisioned, because you wouldn't have picked up this book otherwise. A little healthy skepticism is always a good idea, but staying open to new ideas creates inroads to success. The teacher always arrives when the student is ready.

You're probably wondering who I am, and what I could possibly know, or teach you about pain. That's a fair question, and one we should always ask when we are looking at getting support from someone we don't know. I'm the same: if someone hasn't been in my shoes before, or been down and out, then how can I trust that they have any idea how to pick themselves up by the bootstraps and get back up again, stronger, and more resilient?

There was a time when I was lost and confused. I was terrified of my own shadow, and didn't know who I was or what I wanted. I had false bravado, smiling on the outside, but sad, fearful, and angry on the inside. My parents divorced when I was 14 and my brother was 6. We had a lot of discord in our home. My brother was diagnosed with Schizoid Affective Disorder at 16. I began overeating, and went from 109 lb to 160 lb in 6 months. I suffered from anxiety attacks and phobias, and disassociated from myself at times, even though it looked from the outside as though I had the perfect life. When I went away to college, I left the house and never returned, except on the occasional visit. It was only through a great deal of introspection, and attending many workshops, classes, training, etc. that I found my authentic self and came to live the life I'd always dreamed of. If I was capable of doing all this, it means that you can, too!

My work as a Health and Fitness life coach is my passion as well as my career, and I have spent the last 40-plus years supporting others in loving themselves, stopping the "beat up cycle" and achieving their goals. I have moved from the depths of despair to a life of gratitude and faith.

In this book, you will find a blueprint to create your inner world the way you want it: much the same way as an architect does when designing the house plans for you to build your dream home.

We will examine your motivations to find out if you are living someone else's dream, or your own. I will ask you questions so you can examine in depth what makes you tick. You can write in this book, or have a separate notebook to answer the questions, which are designed to help you weed out your past problems in order to enable healing and growth. If we keep repeating a pattern, we must identify where it originated, then do a little psychological or emotional surgery to get to the root cause so we can extract it and then let it go.

I'm excited to share this journey with you. It is designed to show you how to take steps to get from A to Z, and enjoy the alphabet soup along the way as you navigate the life you were born to live. Everything is outlined for you, so rest assured, we will address all of your questions and concerns. I am hopeful you will have breakthroughs when you answer some of the questions I will ask you. This is your very own personal workshop and transformational book. Each chapter concludes with a haiku in order to cement new concepts and open inroads to your own internal wisdom.

The magic in this book is YOU! Let me be clear, all the things I share with you are things you have heard a million times before. The difference is, you are ready to hear them now, otherwise, you wouldn't have picked up this book. I am going to tell you another secret: ready? There is *no* secret. That's right, that's the secret. You see, it's always been inside of you, waiting to be watered and nourished so you can grow and flourish into the person you are becoming. A diamond in the rough, if you will, waiting to be chiseled and polished. I am so excited to support you in making these discoveries and living your life, your way.

Sometimes a lightbulb goes on, and it's as though you have never seen these things before, which simply means you are ready to follow your desires and live life from the inside out, rather than the outside in. In other words, listening to the small, intuitive messages that come from within, and acting on them, rather than listening to what other people want from you in order to try and work out what you "should" do.

This idea of what we "should" do may even be subconscious, since the media and technology are constantly bombarding us with external, subliminal messages to try to influence our emotions and decision-making processes.

I am interested in finding out what you want to do, not what you think you "should" do, and I hope you are too. This is where the magic comes in, and life starts taking shape in the way you envision. Please don't confine yourself to what you believe you "should" do. I have another secret for you. Ready to hear it? You might not like it, but it's true. I don't have the answers in this book, but I trust you do! Gone are the days of looking outside of yourself and thinking someone else has the answers.

The answers are inside of you, and always have been, and the magic happens when you heed the call to put yourself front and center in your life. My training as a life coach comes from a Socratic approach: asking the right questions to lead us to those "lightbulb moments." I was certified in 1979 as a Life Coach at MMS (Motivational Management Service) by the "Mother of Life Coaching," Dr. Chérie Carter-Scott. The Socratic steps that we were trained in at MMS are tried and tested, and are connected with the International Coaching Federation (ICF).

The simple, fundamental steps that I will outline in the upcoming chapters are most likely ones you already know, but you are now ready to take time to delve deeper into what has gotten in your way of following them up to now.

As a matter of fact, it's your birthright to live your life your way, and, with the proper tools in your tool chest, you will learn how to unleash your God-given talents and heal the wounds that got you here in the first place.

Whether you cringed or cheered when I said the word "God," if you can put your judgements and preconceived notions of God aside, and substitute whatever you want in its place, you won't let language be a barrier in this book. I was unable to use the word "God" for so many years because organized religion is one of the biggest contributors to fighting amongst people and nations of the world, creating separation rather than unity. The last thing I want to do is separate people from each other. It is my biggest hope that we can come together in unity and love. I do come from a spiritual perspective, and I encourage you to use whatever word resonates with you. Some people use Source, Divinity, Higher Power, The Divine, Superpower, Goddess. Use what works for you.

It will be challenging at times for you to dig into your old patterns and psyche. It will not always be easy. Nothing worth having is, and the journey of life is not travelled in a straight line. I love Steve Jobs's quote:

"You can't connect the dots looking forward; you can only connect them looking backwards. So you have to trust that the dots will somehow connect in your future. You have to trust in something - your gut, destiny, life, karma, whatever. This approach has never let me down, and it has made all the difference in my life."

This book is not only a "how to" book, but a journey into your inner self. We will veer off the beaten track at times. You may get frustrated as you try to cut through some of the nuances of the book that give it meaning and substance, and, if you're anything at all like me, you may want to cut to the chase. Feel free to look to the chapters where the steps are outlined for you from time to time, but I encourage you to do the workbook questions as well, so you can have the breakthroughs that happen through experience and doing.

When watching most sporting events, I don't see one darn nuance of the game, but I go because my husband and kids love it. So I skim through magazines (yes, I admit it), eat my cracker jacks and hot dogs, you get the idea. If you are a football fan in the U.S. you might remember "The Catch," The 49-ers most famous play where Joe Montana threw to Dwight Clark to put them into the Super Bowl in 1981. I happened to be at that famous game and slept through most of it (sorry guys), so I understand if you want to move to the Cliff Notes right away. If you want to, feel free to go directly to the "How To's" and skip to the steps you need, jot notes, and add them to your daily to-do list. In other words, this is your book, so scribble in it, cross things out that don't fit for you, and highlight those that do, or rip out pages and make copies if you want to share something with someone.

Too often, we read books the way we live our lives, and are careful never to make a mistake. Make mistakes! I wish you more mistakes than successes, because that is truly where we learn and grow. If, however, you continue making the same ones over and over again, it's time to take a closer look and see what the underlying cause is. This is often easier said than done.

Once you know what the underlying reasons are, sometimes the mistakes clear up on their own, while with others, it's important you tease apart what is keeping you from what you want. If you can't figure it out on your own, reach out and get the help you need from friends, colleagues, further reading, counseling, specialists, life coaches, etc. Let this book be your springboard and your guide.

Step 1: Finding the True You

Who am I?

This question has been asked through the ages by spiritual teachers and religious leaders, authors, psychologists, etc. It is a fundamental question, and spending a little time on it right now will help you when you begin the process of defining your purpose. If you don't know who you are, how can you decide what you want, or where you want to go? You can't! It's as simple as that. The alternative is to run around like a headless chicken, with absolutely no sense of direction.

Alright, let's do this! Get out your pencil and answer these few questions before you move forward in this book. I can't make you stop and answer these questions, but I do want to impress upon you how important it is that you don't skip over this part of the work, because *it is the basic framework from which all of your future progress will derive.* By taking the time needed and doing a deep dive, you will get the most out of our work together.

I'm going to ask you the same question three times, and I'll explore further once you have answered:

Who are you?

Who are you?

Who are you?

I'm curious as to what you came up with here. Did the question stop you in your tracks, get you confused, worry you might write the wrong answers? Did you make a long list of what you do, who you are to people, where you came from, etc.?

I sent these questions to several clients/friends when I was writing this chapter. It stopped most people in their tracks. It was daunting for them on many levels. Thank you all for taking the time to do this, as it really is insightful and helpful!

Some of the responses I got were:

"I'll have to speak to you as I find your request vague; I require more clarification;" "I don't get it at all. What do you mean, 'who are you?' That could take volumes."

"I'll give it some thought. Write on, sister!"

"I really don't know who I am, succinctly; I am trying to figure it out."

"Who I am now is still in search mode, trying to figure out who I was. And whom I am going to be is still up for grabs, as I continue my therapy."

"I came into this world with intuition, but soon became scared of my shadow, very fearful, and worried a lot about being accepted."

"Always searching for spiritual answers, going to different churches, reading tons of self-help books, going to counseling, looking for answers outside of myself. Who I am now is a spiritual being in a human body, comfortable in my own skin, knowing that I am never alone. I am confident that I am immortal and not fearful of the future."

"Genuine, introspective, adventurous, overthinker, empathetic, sensitive, easy to laugh with, both love and hate change, cynical and idealistic."

*"Journeywoman, striving, tired.
Struggling, growing, grateful.
Learning, loving, peace-seeker.
Lover, learner, creator."*

I love of all these answers, and, as you can see, it is a question that most of us struggle with, or maybe have never given any thought to at all. The responses above came from people who are 20–92 years of age, from a range of different backgrounds, beliefs, and genders.

Some of us have never been asked this question or taken the time to look introspectively at what comes up for us when we ask it.

We stop, because it stops us in our tracks if we have never been confronted with such a fundamental question.

The other thing that happens is, we think there is a "right" answer, and this immobilizes us, which is quite normal, and it happens to me as well. I think most of us have a similar reaction.

If you said, "I'll come back to this later," I suggest you do it now or put a date on your calendar to make sure you come back to it.

I'm going to share my own responses with you, but I hope you will write yours down before you read mine, so you can gain your own insights.

Who am I?

I am a mother, wife, daughter, friend, niece, aunt, sister-in-law, chauffeur, dog- and cat-ma, soon to be grandma, Health and Wellness coach, Yoga teacher, confidante, chef, writer of words and poetry, cleaner, designer, breadwinner, loving, kind, compassionate, obsessive, a workaholic, getting old, an environmentalist, introspective, creative, patient, impatient, flexible, tight, creative.

I'm an adventurist, optimist, caregiver, reader, blogger, malleable, judgmental, curious, intolerant, outraged, vocal, silent, contemplative, honest, truthful, clearer, have more boundaries, guilt-ridden,

Who am I?

I am older, wiser, slower, vibrant, wrinkled, my eyes are drier, a prune, strong, weak, impatient, intolerant, tolerant, tired, open, clearer, for the people, unifier, deaf, blind, compassionate, passionate, frustrated, joyful, resentful.

Who am I?

I am light, love, spirit, truth, principle, soul, joy, the stars, the moon, divinity, oneness, whole, broken, fractured, healing, Becoming, essence, insightful, introspective, open, changing, listening, spirit, love, truth, nothing, everything, divinity, love, I am love, I am love, I am love. I just am.

What generally happens for me, no matter how many times I do this, is that I start out answering all the things I *do*, rather than who I *am* at my core. We often define ourselves by what we have done rather than who we are, deep within. We learn from an early age that we get approval for what we *do*. Often, our list becomes a resume of things we have done. We never know who we are, as we continue to add a whole host of credentials to our name. Some credentials are important and impressive, for sure, but who we are is not what we have done in our lives.

Often, we think we are what people have told us we are, but we don't know who we truly are.

Let me digress. I have a dear friend who always says, "we don't like this, that or the other thing," when she refers to her large family of nine. This always blows my mind. Growing up, at the time I was a child, we didn't have as many choices. When we were served food, or anything else for that matter, we just ate it, or did what we were told, without complaining.

Nowadays, we give children so many choices that they can't decide on basic things half of the time. I know I was guilty of that when I raised my kids, which might be the reason that I have everyone eating different things according to their specific needs. I ended up working double-time. Live and learn. There is value in both. Teaching children to discern what they like and don't like is important, but too many choices can leave them confused, never really finding out what they like, or what they want.

Back on point, we are not what other people tell us we are. Often, we let others define us without checking in with ourselves. We take a role in the family, so we can have our own identity, and continue on that track without question, so we can keep the peace, and not create a problem for others. A life without question keeps us repeating the past, which may not serve us anymore. Living for others is a life without knowing who we are, and unfulfilling at the very least. When we are so busy being who others want us to be for their convenience and approval, we can lose sight of ourselves.

The age-old question of "Who am I?" is one that most of us struggle with, because we were never raised with someone asking us this question, or with them reflecting their own solid essence of who *they* were, on *us*.

When we were born, we entered the world with a clean slate, and perhaps other lifetimes that have come with us, or perhaps just our own ancestry and family DNA. It is important we learn how to tease apart what is truly *us*, versus what has been handed down to us.

Many of us are given a set of moral codes, ethics, dogmas, expectations, etc., depending on where we are born, our ethnic background, religious or spiritual beliefs, caste, or creed. Many of us are taught to follow a set of guidelines, all of which help give structure to our day. We are sent to school (if we are lucky), pressured to live up to high expectations and grades, to be an integral part of our families, and to contribute and bring pride to our family name. Sometimes it's hard, if not impossible, to break out of what our family heritage is, because we haven't had any choice in the matter.

There is no fairness in this, but it is what it is. We need to adapt to our environment, or we will end up swimming upstream for the rest of our lives. We need to understand what we are dealing with, so we can find ways to make our life our own, and bring about the changes we want to see in the world, as difficult as this sounds.

Let me be clear, where we come from is not who we are. It is what has been imprinted upon us, and it is our job to look beyond the surface and dig deeper. At our core, we are all the same, truly. We all get up every morning and put our legs into our pants on our own, or with assistance, but none of us escape the daily living requirements of being human.

Who are we not?

We are not our material possessions, what we buy, what we eat, where we go, where we live, how much money we make, what adjectives we have come up with to describe ourselves, what we do for a living, what hobbies we have, what we are good at, what we are bad at, our ego, what we believe, our opinions, our feelings, our bodies, what people tell us we are, or who we think we are.

So, who are we then?

You may have noticed that the more you did this exercise, the more you got down to the essence of your being. When I say your being, I simply mean who you are in essence. Our mind likes us to think that our thoughts are who we are, but the mind is simply the computer in the brain that judges, analyzes, and figures things out.

What did you find?

What I have come to know over years of trying to discover who I am is simply *I am*. I am beyond thought and feeling, the essence of love and light, and so are you. This is truly who we all are if we strip ourselves of all the labels we have taken on in life. At the risk of sounding airy fairy, there is a stillness and a softness that reflects through our inner being and radiates out through our aura. How we access this daily can become difficult when we have so much to do. We can be transformed into a human *doing* rather than a human *being* in no time at all. Therefore, it is vital to connect with our inner being, moment to moment. It is also vital that we give time and attention to ourselves, and not overload ourselves with things that don't matter, and simply take up space and time.

You might ask, "if we are all light and love, then what about all of the evil in this world? How is it possible?" While we all suffer from the effects of those who only seek personal gain at the expense of others, we cannot lose sight of the truth that such people have truly never learned the principles we are discussing here, because they are so deeply wounded. This is a topic for another book (and many books have been written on the subject), so I will simply say that we need to hold the light for all beings, everywhere, and draw the line so justice can be found.

Climbing The Ladder

So, if we are love and light at our deepest level, why do we keep trying to get to the top of the ladder, and loath when we fall off, or are halfway there? What is this urgency inside to get where we are going? Is it just ego, or is there something internal that is driving us? It is important to look behind the curtain to find out what drives us. As much as we are spiritual beings living in a physical body, we are still humans. We need to stop and look at our motives before they take over, and we end up following without question. A life without question is like a life lived in a maze, running after the cheese when we prefer chocolate. If we don't stop and look inside at what we are doing, we are simply captive on the same treadmill, racing to get somewhere when we aren't even sure what we want. We were once hunters, gatherers and nesters, and that fight-or-flight impulse is deeply ingrained in our programing, even if we no longer have lions and tigers and bears at our doorstep.

I see all kinds of people, and I can assure you that what you *have* doesn't necessarily make you happier. We accumulate possessions, and soon become slaves to them. More toys, more to keep track of and pay for. It perpetuates the age-old lie that *more is better.* We keep thinking, "when we get *here* or there or achieve *this goal,* all of our issues will be solved," but that just isn't the case. See more about this in Step 4, Plan of Action.

Weeding Ourselves Out from Others

Do you ever wonder if who you are is your mother, father, grandparents, or siblings?

While it's true that the DNA of our ancestors runs deep, it is not *who we are*, but a part of our overall system.

When we are in utero, we are completely dependent on our mothers for our nourishment and sustenance. The umbilical cord is attached to our mother's uterus, which is where all our food gets broken down and fed to us to create all of our organs and systems. So, what she ingests is vital for the healthy development of our bodies on a cellular level. We also pick up on all of her feelings and emotions, and this has an impact upon us. If we had a mother who was constantly stressed, or in fear, the adrenaline and dopamine get transferred to us as well. If you are pregnant and this just triggered you into worrying about your baby because you had a negative thought or emotion, stop right there. This is a normal part of pregnancy, because your hormones are adjusting on many levels, something over which you have no control. I remember worrying that if I was crying or angry, that my baby would carry all of this. I consulted many pregnant moms when I was teaching pre/postnatal classes who felt the same way. We cannot deny our feelings. If we try to, it is unhealthy, because we set up a negative feedback loop in our brains and start obsessing, which can literally drive us crazy. Creating as serene of an environment as possible, full of love and joy, is helpful when you are pregnant. Honoring exactly where you are is crucial as well.

There is a symbiotic connection between mother and child: they are one during and after birth in their bond and connection. The baby is dependent on her for his or her sole existence, both emotionally and physically, which can be overwhelming for the mom if she is not getting the emotional and physical support she needs so she can care for her baby. Slowly, they begin to separate, and ideally create healthy attachments with others independent from each other, which is vital, so the baby can grow into a healthy independent being separate from his or her mother. If you are a mother, you know that this is one of the hardest things to do, because you love your child so much and want the best for them. Letting go is one of the hardest things to do, and generally for the mother because she carried the child. "We carry them for nine months, and we carry them on our backs for the rest of our lives," as the saying goes.

We gift our children independence as we continue to see them separate from us, and let them make their own choices. When there is a lot of fear and angst, and the desire to control because it is so hard to let go, separation is fraught with difficulties.

My mom and dad married at 18 and 20 years old. My mom had me at 20, both, "not wet behind the ears," as I heard my father say many times. They were babies themselves. They had sex for the first time on their honeymoon, which is rather rare today. Both were working, independent, movie-star gorgeous, young, and still had a lot of growing up to do. I was the apple of my mom's eye, as she tells the story of the nurses bringing me in to her saying, "here is your little Audrey Hepburn." My claim to fame!

When we have a child, there is a lot of deferred gratification, and there needs to be some maturity on the part of both parents. The woman may not be interested in having sex anytime soon. I mean seriously, when a bowling ball comes out of a hole the size of a pea, can you blame her?

My father did not have the maturity nor impulse control to abstain from sex, and ended up having many affairs, which crushed my mother. They tried for years to have another baby, and finally my brother was born eight years later. They stayed together for another five years after that. It was a struggle for my mom to raise us as a single mom, working full time. She remarried not long afterwards, and had some good years, but as history tends to repeat itself, it was a tumultuous marriage at best.

Our children got the best part of my stepfather, for which I will be eternally grateful. They say a generation removed makes up for a lot of pain and contentiousness, and I would have to agree. We had four children within six years, so life was busy, which kept me from looking inside at my needs while I made sure everyone was clothed, fed, and loved. Every time I contemplated having another baby, I would ask my mom if she was ready, and she said a resounding "yes!" If it weren't for her, I would probably have stopped at three. I don't know what I would have done without her.

She had a lot of fears, insecurities and sadness that she harbored well, yet were transferred over to me, which I would say when she was pregnant with me.

I had many phobias that I hid from the world around me. I honestly thought I was crazy for most of my life, despite how successful I was in the world at large. I prayed a lot, diverted, and distracted myself to keep my feelings at bay, took on more work than was good for me, and was always looking for approval. I became a chameleon, and morphed into whomever anyone wanted me to be, which gave me a false sense of bravado. I also developed ways to disconnect from myself, so I could find sanity. My mother needed me, and I couldn't disappoint her. She had so much more to deal with than me. She was raising my brother, who had schizophrenia. In my mind, I was his second mother. I always wished I could do something more to help him, and tried to the best of my ability, but with our age gap so large and me busy being a teenager, trying to figure my own life, I did the best I could. She was an amazing mother. She was loving, caring and always had food on the table. There was abundance at every birthday and holiday, with lavish parties, but she didn't have the emotional support she needed, having grown up in a dysfunctional family with three siblings. I wasn't beaten or molested. We went to church, and along with the fighting, there was always a lot of laughter, but I was lost: confused and split off from myself, trying to find a place in the world.

As you can imagine, it was hard for my mom to let go when I left for college. She never really let me go, nor I, her. She was my best friend and confidante. I told her everything, even at that age. I was a goodie-two-shoes, and was grounded for "sassing off," but that's about all I can remember that I did wrong. I never lied, drank, snuck out, or even took a puff of a cigarette, yet walked to the store most nights to get a pack of cigarettes for her with a note she signed for permission to sell them to me. Sometimes I was terrified walking home in the dark, and I would run to the porches of our neighbors' houses if I saw a car coming, even though we lived in a good neighborhood.

When I got to college to meet my new roommate, I'll never forget her answering the door cutting something white. At first I thought it was sugar, and that she was making tea or lemonade (that's how naïve I was), and when I found out it was cocaine, I nearly freaked out. My mother told me never to take drugs, and I listened to her as she was God in my eyes, and put the fear of God in me as well. She said, "if you take LSD or anything like that, you could jump off a building or become crazy" and I certainly didn't want to feel any crazier than I already felt.

My roommate, who is to this day one of my best friends, said, "you are so much fun, I want you to try marijuana as you will be even more fun." I was skeptical, to say the least, but finally said, "Alrighty, I'll give it a go." I called my mom and let her know I was going to try it, and promised I would call her the next day. She was a nervous wreck, but I stood my ground and after all I was paying for all of my college, dorm living and food, so she had no leg to stand on.

While everyone around me was laughing, I sat there like a bump on the log. The next day my roommate said, "never do this again" to which I agreed, of course.

I called my mom, and she was so relieved I hadn't jumped off a bridge somewhere. My kids, however, have this idea that I was a complete hippy when I was growing up, which I sadly missed. Maybe since I burn incense and chant and some of my friends were true hippies, they don't believe me. When I look back, I think I would have done some crazy and wild things if I could change things, but my mom did keep me safe from substance abuse, for which I'm grateful.

 When I had kids, I thought they would just listen to me, like I did my mom, which was the farthest thing from the truth. They gave me a run for my money, sneaking out, drinking alcohol, smoking, and trying drugs. All but one, I should say, to set the record straight. Every time we busted them, there were consequences, but I just couldn't figure out how they would disobey me. I look back and wonder how I could have been so naïve, which just shows how sheltered I was. They say they will be smarter when they have kids since they know all the tricks. Some will be stricter and some less strict, and I say, "good luck!"

My mom confided so many of her struggles, and some of the horrible things that had happened to her, including almost being molested.

Somehow, I thought all of what happened to her had also happened to me. When I found out in later years that it didn't happen to me but her, I was in shock, and it also alleviated a lot of my unfounded fears. I didn't know where she ended, and where I began, and I was carrying all of this around, which is an example of how symbiotic relationships work, and the necessity of letting go and breaking away, so we can be our own independent selves.

I tell you this story so you might look at your own life and discern what is yours, and what is someone else's, so you are able to create healthy boundaries.

It was later in life that I finally separated myself from my mother for the sake of my own sanity. This was very hurtful to her, because she had come to depend on our relationship, but the need to find out who I was, and who I was not, was eating me alive. When we live for others and not ourselves, we do a disservice to both people.

I will talk more about weeding out what choices you are making based on someone else's wishes versus your own in Step 3: Finding Your *Want* and *Why*.

This is a lot of information to take in, I know, but it is important for you to do some soul-searching, especially if you are still trying to figure out who you really are.

Go back and do the exercise, *"Who am I?"* many times, and see how you continue to pierce through the layers, until you reach your authentic self:

> *Layer by layer*
> *peeling back the masks we wear*
> *reveal hidden truth*

Step 2: Finding Your Purpose

Finding your purpose is the key to living a happy, joyful, and fulfilling life. Without purpose, we sail in a direction that takes us away from ourselves, rather than towards ourselves, leaving us empty, or always climbing a ladder of success so we can finally feel whole and connected. However, this doesn't always pan out, and deep down, we know if we believe in it or not. Many of us suffer from Imposter Syndrome, which is loosely defined as doubting your abilities and feeling like a fraud. It disproportionately affects high-achieving people. It can play out in either a positive or negative way, if we aren't aware of what is going on in our unconscious mind.

If we feel deserving, then we will create abundance, and windows of opportunity will open to us. If we don't, the opposite will happen.

All great leaders know what their purpose is, and where they want to go, and chart a course with a plan of how to get there, enlisting support and help from others they may need. "No man is an island," as the saying goes, and the support and expertise of others can help us chart our path successfully.

"Act as if, and it will follow" is sound advice, and very true, especially when we are new at something, and need to build traction and self-esteem. In time, we will "get it" but in the meantime, we can't let the mind take over, since it is designed to overanalyze and judge everything we do. If we listen to the voice of self-doubt, we will never get our first sale, so to speak.

What if I told you that your purpose was already inside of you, and all you needed to do was chisel and polish the diamond in the rough that you already are? Imagine if that were your only job? It sounds so easy, and it is. I'm not saying there won't be obstacles: there will be, that is part of life. I'm saying we need to know what drives us, who we are, and what is important for us to do in the world, in order to satisfy our soul in this lifetime.

To be clear, purpose is *not* a goal or an objective, but the guiding force that leads us toward a life of true fulfillment. It is what gives us the fire in our bellies, much the same way that a car needs a battery pack to run. It also needs to be recharged, just as we do. A purpose in and of itself isn't enough: we need to know what makes us tick, and what we are here to do in the world. When we know truly what that is, a magic portal opens inside of us, and we align with our mission in life. Without it, we flail like a fish out of water, trying to find its breathing gills.

There is something you came into the earth to do. Do you know what it is?

Purpose is your life's foundation: just as a house needs a solid foundation, you need a sound body, mind, and spirit in order to thrive.

You are reading this book because you have come to a point in your life where you want to live beyond the surface: where each day is a gift of the heart, opening pathways deep within yourself in order to discover and be who you are meant to be.

Every age and stage offers new insights and opportunities to adapt and change: we have never been at this place in our lives before, so it's important to pause and ask, "who am I now, and what is my purpose?"

As we continue to grow, we face new challenges that we must adjust to in order to make room for change. Change is not always easy, but it is inevitable, and if we get set in our ways, we can hinder our growth, and our ability to open to our highest good. In much the same way as meditation, we need to practice this acceptance of change, so it is accessible when we want to draw upon it.

Staying open to what *is*, instead of relying on what *was*, keeps us flexible and calm instead of rigid and easy to break.

I do a daily movement in tai chi called "wave hands like clouds" to remind me that, like the clouds, things come and go, and nothing ever stays the same. I also try to take new routes when I walk or drive, to make better use of my cognitive senses and I suggest you do this as well. I often get lost, which my family can attest to, but it gives me the opportunity to calm my anxiety and become more resourceful.

Take time with this chapter to truly familiarize yourself with the spirit that drives you, and gives meaning to your life.

At the age of 10, we wonder.

At 20, we imagine.

At 30, we cogitate.

At 40, we think.

At 50, we have an idea or two.

At 60, we have two ideas.

At 70, we are working towards one idea.

At 80 plus, we realize, and wonder if we ever knew anything at all.

Author unknown, but this was included in a speech that my uncle and grandfather wrote together when my uncle came in second place at the San Joaquin speaking contest for all of the high schools in that county. My father has memorized and can recite the entire speech they wrote to this day.

My grandfather used to hold family court, at which each family member would have to recite poetry, give speeches and sing. This would take place weekly after dinner. It was a ritual in which we would all participate when we would gather in later years, and most likely where my children got their incredible presence both on and off the stage. It has certainly helped them land top jobs in their chosen industries. The ability to think on their feet, field executive decisions creatively, and speak with confidence is truly magnificent.

Unfortunately, my grandfather died at 64, and his other brothers also died of heart attacks around the same time: way too young. However, his message of opening to the daily gifts life provides continues to teach us to thrive and stay present. My father and aunt continued this tradition. My aunt just died at 92, and my dad and is still alive and well after changing his diet and reducing his stress level. In spite of his many health challenges, he continues to entertain us with incredible stories and poems he's memorized over the years, or will break out into song walking down the street. He recites poems and speeches fluently that he's memorized, which is more than likely where I got my love of people, sports, writing and creativity. We cringe at his braggadocio (and we're not Italian) but admire his spirit and zest for life.

His favorite story was singing to Marilyn Monroe in I. Magnin Department Store in San Francisco and getting fired. To this day he carries her picture in his pocket and drops it as he walks by a woman, saying, "excuse me, you dropped something", which was his favorite pick-up line. We've heard it so many times that we roll our eyes to the back of our heads. He was tall, blonde and handsome, the lead in high school plays, an amazing athlete in baseball, basketball and tennis, and played with some top athletes. One time we were on vacation when I was young, and he had a flock of women lined up outside the door to get his autograph because they thought he was Troy Donahue, an American film and television actor and singer.

Sadly, my dad's family had a lot of ego and false bravado. He was rarely around when I was growing up, or when he was, I was dragged to the tennis courts while he played, and I watched, sat politely as a wallflower saying "please" and "thank you." I rarely saw him after my parents' divorce when I was 14. The abandonment issues stemming from him forgetting to pick me up for an outing, or never coming to any of my school events, took a long time to heal from, but this is probably where I formed my life purpose, which I constantly adjust and re-define.

Remember, before you can come up with your *want* and *why* goals and aspirations, you have to know who you are, and identify your underlying purpose: what you are here in this world to do.

Even when you are sure of your purpose, you can occasionally veer off track. This means that life is trying to tell you something: don't let it throw you off kilter, but rather teach you more about yourself and your motivations, one step at a time.

Here are the questions to ask yourself to help you discover your purpose *now*. Go ahead, write in your book, or keep a separate journal nearby to jot things down that come up as you shed light on who you are, and begin to find your purpose.

1. **What is your overall purpose?**

2. **What did you come to earth to do?**

3. **Why is this important to you?**

4. **What role did/do you have in your family?**

5. **Is this role one you want to keep?**

6. **What makes your heart sing?**

7. **How can you stay aligned with your purpose every day?**

What life is worth living that is not worth questioning?

Life is precious and pure in its essence. It is messy and fragile in its execution, and we must call on all aspects of the Divine in order to survive. We have a choice to either paint rainbows or black clouds on our blank canvas. We must walk amongst all of life's colors and know that we are none of them. We must throw away the script we have been given, and ab lib our lives like an actor on the screen, bringing forth our true nature, which may have been long hidden beneath the surface.

Welcome to a new way of living your life: authentically, and in alignment with the reason you were put here on this earth. I'm excited to share your journey with you.

Sit still in the quietness of your own mind. Let the stillness invite questions. You are worth the time. Slow your breathing and notice the physical sensations as it slows down. Feel the softness between the rough edges of your psyche. Accept the feelings of impatience which stem from wanting to suppress your feelings in order to escape them.

If not now, when?

Once you discover your purpose, everything falls into place, and you can stand on your own two feet with true satisfaction, rather than empty promises. No one can take it away from you, no matter how many times you fall, lose, or are embarrassed or bruised, as you have learned resilience and now know how to pick yourself up and start over, again and again, for as many times as it takes.

Nirvana Found

The lake glistens, reflecting gray and white shadows, while the birds drift with the tide.
The great blue heron
sits patiently, waiting to score a fish.
There is no trying to be patient, trying to be present, trying to be still without his mind racing, he just is.

I am jealous of his ability, while I sit cross-legged in meditation, thoughts bombarding my mind while my body aches with the strain.

I want to be the blue heron and dive into the water, unafraid if I get cold or wet, not worrying whether I catch a fish every time. Unbothered by what time it is, what I must do, how I will pay the bills, where I'm supposed to be in an hour, who I might offend if I say my truth; not worrying if I stay in bed all day and just watch him and the shimmering water.

For a moment, I become one with the blue heron, and I'm still, content, and quiet inside.
Nirvana found.

But for now, there are chores to do and places to be, so I will *drag myself from the windowsill. I take a picture in my mind's eye so I can return to this memory throughout my day.*

When you know what your purpose is, you will move mountains. I always felt deep inside that my purpose was to serve. If I look at my family background, expectations, and the unconscious contract I made with my family, I can see from a psychological perspective, that I was expected to take care of the family.

The trauma was so deep, that I felt it was my job to take care of others in the hopes that if I did, they would finally see me, and I would get the love and attention I deserved. I needed this to feel whole, as every child does. This is what was going on in my unconscious mind, and I didn't realize it until years later. It's what gave me a job and a purpose in the family, my career, my parenting, my friendships etc., even though it was killing me on the inside, and this didn't show up until years later.

Children often mistake their parents' shortcomings for their own, when this is far from the truth. They will continue the role they have been assigned, in order to keep peace with those around them, at the expense of themselves.

This conditioning runs deep, and when children start to uncover these truths, many lash out and blame others for their shortcomings. They may be angry at the role they have taken on in order to save face and try to find peace. Their intentions are good, but their actions don't bring satisfaction or healing either to themselves or their loved ones.

When we can see the truth that it was *not* our problem or our job to fix those around us, we can escape this chamber of hell. At the time we were growing up, this behavior may have been important for our survival, and it served us well. But unless we examine the underlying cause, we will continue to be trapped. In the words of Socrates, "The unexamined life is not worth living."

Even though your situation might still be the same, knowing where you start and someone else ends is crucial to maintaining your sense of self. Therein lies the problem. How do you discern this when you have been brainwashed into thinking you need nothing, and your job is to take care of everyone? This is where the inner work becomes essential, so you can separate out what belongs to you and what belongs to another person, on an emotional level. When you see things for what they are, you can begin to know your own mind, and drop others' opinions of who you are, and what you need to do. You begin to put yourself front and center. This is not easy, I know, and harder for some than others, but it is ultimately what will set you free from the prison of expectation.

My family looked perfect from the outside, but on the inside, it was a dysfunctional mess, not unlike a lot of families we all know, or are part of. I took on the role of savior in order to create peace, trying to take care of everyone, and working overtime to please everyone with the hope that someone would finally see me, and then perhaps I wouldn't have to work that hard.

After years of trying to take care of everyone and falling apart on the inside, I began to question the assumption that any of this was my fault, and realized it was my job to take care of myself (as selfish as this felt), so I could put Humpty Dumpty back together again, and let others either fall apart or rise to the occasion and take care of their own needs.

The life we've been given is not necessarily the one we've wanted, but it is the life which has enabled us to find our purpose. Does that make sense?

I wish that I and everyone else would have come into a loving environment free from friction, dysfunction, and hardship, but that would have robbed me and you of the lessons we needed to learn to arrive at a place of acceptance, gratitude, and love.

Was I jealous of those who came into families that were intact, and didn't have to work that hard? Of course I was! I remember some of my friends whose parents were together and weren't fighting, or there wasn't the covert anger that was seething under the surface like in my family. I remember some of my friends getting all 'A's and not having to work hard, while I struggled to get 'B's or 'C's. I remember my friends who had their whole college paid for, while I had to work to pay for mine. I had a roof over my head and clothes which my mom worked hard to provide, but to say I wasn't envious would be a lie. That is a normal human emotion.

Some people came into the world without having to prove themselves, and could leave all the wasted energy of being something for someone else behind, so they could pursue their goals and find their purpose, seemingly without stress or struggle. Unfortunately, many of us did not. While this is ideal, the truth is, we never know what is truly going on inside another person and how they really feel versus the persona they show to the world in order to protect themselves, or to save face. Just look at social media and how people spin things to inflate their egos.

With that said, these very people we envied also had their own set of obstacles and challenges to face, as life offers no one a free ride, and those that think otherwise are in for some surprises along the way. The child born with a silver spoon never learns to feed himself, as the saying goes. I see it every day. Those with more material possessions have more to worry about, and more guilt at feeling like they don't deserve what they have. The constructs they build for protection are even bigger, and the guilt, pain and internal struggle can seem insurmountable.

On the contrary, if you are born with nothing, on the streets, cold, broke, and starving with no role model, you do whatever you can to survive. Our world isn't fair, and we deal with this either by trying to help, or closing our eyes to it, because it feels insurmountable.

Many times, we become the victim of our situation. Instead of digging in and getting the help we need, we stick with the same set of circumstances, and we can never get out of this loophole because we haven't learned to pick ourselves up by our bootstraps and take responsibility for our problems. The familiarity of victimhood is safer and more comfortable, so we continue the same cycle of repetition, never getting off the merry-go-round. Merry-go-rounds are supposed to be fun, so jump on, dig in, and find your way.

Find what makes your heart sing and what you were born to share. Notice I didn't say, "do." *Doing* often gets us in trouble, and we become like drones, moving without ever wondering why, and never stopping to breathe in the essence of the moment afforded by our experience, enjoying our surroundings and the gifts of Mother Earth.

At birth, we are full of wonder, and everything is new. We come from a black and white world to one full of color and noise, faces and experiences. We learn how to adapt to our surroundings.

As we grow, our young years are consumed by trying to fit in, making friends, and figuring out where we begin and end.

During our teens, we break out, searching for independence, and adopt a know-it-all approach, often defying parental and other adult opinions. We often receive backlash from our parents and other authorities, and we rebel.

At 18, or college age, we continue to experience and explore our newfound rights, and test the waters.

At 20-30, we may start our own families, and began to experience commitment, finding some independence from our parents. We begin to find our own power and take responsibility for our lives, at least monetarily speaking, building our own nest, and perhaps having children of our own.

Of course, many adults choose not to get married or have children. Others explore their own sexuality and gender, and speak up about how they identify themselves in the world.

But this isn't who you are either!

Who you are is divine light and love, on a fundamental level, and there is something you are here to teach the world that also fulfills you.

After the cement has filled in the cracks and added a layer of kintsugi, we share our experience and life lessons with the world.

My own purpose is to be as true to my inner callings as I can, so I can support and encourage others to do the same.

Now, whatever I do comes from this place, and shows up in ways that I might not understand entirely at this moment.

But as I continue to follow my inner callings, new pathways open in my life's journey.

I remember when I first felt this deep love and elation. I wanted to run to a mountain top and scream, "Love yourself first, you are enough!" and, in my euphoria, I thought I could be Gandhi and save the world. My next shout out was, "Stop this crazy making and killing; peace is within our jurisdiction!"

I spent the next several years of my life trying to shout that message from the rooftops, until I finally landed into a big heap of disillusionment, realizing the only one I could save was myself. I have never seen a nerve break down, but I'm sure we could find a neurologist to explain the process. Hitting rock bottom and breaking the disillusionment and disassociation that comes with it creates new opportunities for learning and growth, once we recover from the initial shock.

The steps to finding our own inner purpose, and the ability to see people as they are and accept them for the lives they choose, is essential to our spiritual growth. I realized I was not capable of changing or helping anyone who did not in fact want to help themselves. Painful as this is, it is the only true way to be of service: acknowledging that change must come from within, and we can only change ourselves.

Now it's your turn. Did anything pop out at you? It might take you a little time to define your purpose but get out your pen and give it ago. I suggest you do it at least once every year as you continue on your path at different ages and stages.

What is my purpose?

1.

2.

3.

4.

5.

6.

7.

8.

9.

10.

Now narrow this down to one overall purpose. Have fun with this! You can't fail. This is your life after all, and you get to decide. Every one of us has our very own special stamp of why we are here, and what we are here to do.

You might define it a few different ways. To give you a sense of this, here are some examples of what others have found:

*Defining what gives your life meaning and satisfaction.
Perhaps it is reaching your goals and objectives.
Entertaining the world by acting, singing dancing, writing to entertain and bring laughter, love or hope.*

Maybe it's being a reflection of what you stand for and what you want your legacy to be. It's important it brings you joy, health, love and happiness.

My personal purpose has changed over the years.

I remember when I wanted to be Gandhi and "help the world." I realized that this was too much weight for me to hold, because I am only human, as much as I am as spiritual being living in a physical body. I cannot change the world in its entirety. I can only change *me*, and in doing that, I am able to support others in finding their own purpose and solutions to their problems.

I redefine this every year by trial and error.

My current purpose at this time, age and stage is:

To take such good care of me, that I can be a reflection for others to do the same and empower them to live the life they want to have.

*Stay grounded in self
listen with all your senses
open to insight.*

Step 3: Finding Your *Want* and *Why*

Now that you have identified your purpose, what is your *want* and *why*? It's vital to know your *want* and *why*, because without knowing what they are, it's as if you are building a house without a foundation, or a set of plans. It's essential to take time to look at your deeper motivation. It must be big enough, in order to attain your intended goal. If it isn't, you will most likely flounder, or chase aspirations that are simply whims. It is the blueprint that gives your desires a sure footing to propel you forward so you don't fizzle out before you start.

For example, you might want to lose weight for an upcoming wedding you are attending. You may or may not reach your goal.

The first question to ask yourself when you come to your *want* and *why* is, "who is this for?" Is it truly for yourself, or is it for someone else? Is it really your dream, or is it a dream someone else has for you? Rarely does it succeed if it's for someone else. You can grow resentment over time, or, even if you achieve your goal, you will never have the satisfaction you are looking for if it's not for you.

I'll give you an example. My Mother always wanted me to be

a Job's Daughter, and on the marching team for them. Her sister and brother-in-law were Eastern Stars at the Masonic temple in San Francisco. She wanted me to be part of the organization for all the right reasons, but the trouble was, it wasn't something I necessarily wanted, but I did it for her. She was a single mom at the time, raising two children, and she wanted a good foundation for me, with moral values that could sustain me. I marched on the drill team, winning 1st place at convention, and marched in the Columbus Day Parade in San Francisco every year. I was the 3rd messenger, went to the dances they had organized and had some friends, but I always felt like a fish out of water.

Later, she wanted me to run for Miss Daly City, which is a small town just out of San Francisco where I grew up. In this way she could claim her fame. Although both of my parents came from a middle-class family and worked hard to make ends meet, my Dads's brother was a famous and wealthy lawyer living in Burlingame, California. This was going to give her the clout she wanted to fit into that world. I in fact did win Miss Daly City, and when I showed up for the next pageant, The Dream Girl Pageant in the county, it just so happened my cousin had won Miss Burlingame and was competing against me. Imagine the shock of finding that out that I had family competition for both me and my mom.

At that moment, I decided I was done, but continued forward in order to live out the dream my mom had for me. The trouble is it was her dream, not mine. I'll never forget gaining the weight back and deciding then and there that it was enough for me. I really couldn't care less, but was encouraged to continue. Dropping out was not ever an option in my life. We were taught to complete what we started, which did have its merits. I have a vivid memory of walking across the stage, lifting my stomach in, smiling ear to ear with a phony bravado and thinking, "I have to win" and give it my best shot, knowing full well it was too late, but I knew my job was to save face, and I couldn't fail her. Competition was born in our bones, and it was our job to win at any cost, no matter the internal damage. Sure enough, I lost, and my cousin came in 2nd runner-up. My mother to this day says it was political and rigged, and it might have been, but I knew in my bones, this was her dream not mine. The girl who was first runner-up remains one of my best friends to this day, which was the silver lining, and an example of knowing your *why*. When you are young, you may not have a choice, but you can learn from those times when you had to do what was expected of you, rather than what you wanted.

Athletes who are groomed for winning often spend the rest of their lives in the shadows, living out their parents' dreams while unhappy on the inside. Tiger Woods is a perfect example: groomed to be an athlete and follow in his father's footsteps. As good as he is, he had a long, painful process to move through. So many of us think that if we were famous, rich, had a fancy car, house, and perfect body, we would have the perfect life. All you need to do is look at the tabloids to see that this is as far from the truth as possible.

In the past, you may have set your goals, clarified your intention, and made a plan of action, but you fell short of reaching them. Why? It's an important question to ask, so you can find out what has happened to derail you.

Have you clarified the reason that this goal is important to you? This is the biggest reason for success or failure. Without a true desire that is in alignment with your higher purpose, it becomes an empty wish. What is *your* why?

Take some time to see if what you say you want is truly for you, or if it is to please someone else. It can be anything from wanting to go on a trip, wanting a new car, a new job, losing weight, getting in shape, getting healthier, being on time, breaking off a relationship, going to the moon, being free of anxiety, depression, negative self-talk, shyness, obsessions, PTSD, addiction to alcohol, drugs, etc. Truly, this is *your* dream, so you get to choose. Write down anything and everything without filtering it. This is your list, and you get to play and have fun with it. It also doesn't have to make sense; it just must feel right. Never mind the obstacles that will get in the way when you think of them, or the negative self-talk you might hear in your head. That's just your mind, which is designed to analyze and tell you why things can't, or won't, work. If you hear things like. "What are you thinking? You can't do that, you have bills to pay, you already chose a career, you've tried to change before, and you haven't been successful, so this won't work," etc., you can be sure you are on the right track.

I would encourage you to stop for a minute right now and

make a list of 7 things you really want to do. Go ahead and write them down.

1.

2.

3.

4.

5.

6.

7.

Now look and make certain these are what you really want, and they aren't for someone else.

Write next to them why you want whatever it is you said you wanted.

Is this to prove something?

Is it to measure up to someone else's desires for you?

Will it give you fulfillment or status?

What is important to you?

The top things I hear people want are to lose weight; get up early; go to bed early; hit the gym; meditate; practice yoga; stop stressing; stop procrastinating; be on time; end a toxic relationship; eat healthier; take their supplements; stop watching so much television; limit screen games and drinking mid-week. Sometimes the list is so long it's overwhelming.

Pick one, and start with that! After clarifying your goals, you need to create a plan of action with dates to achieve them, and then create a support system to help you stay on track.

Feeling unworthy can prevent you from keeping your word with yourself, and desire isn't enough. Do you keep complaining about not reaching what it is you say you want? When your mind/ego wins out by giving negative attention for not following through, you create a negative feedback loop. The negative attention you give to the problem perpetuates this downward cycle and the mind and ego are at least happy to get some form of attention even if it's negative, crazy as this sounds. Beating yourself up becomes a familiar pattern of massaging addictive behavior. The mind doesn't care if it's getting negative or positive attention, as long as it's getting attention, so take note. It is cunning and ruthless. This is all the more reason to emphasize the positive attention, in order to drown out the negative.

Make sure this goal is something *you* want for yourself, not what someone else wants for you. That never has enough staying power.

Reaching your goals becomes a question of, "How can you love yourself enough to create what you want?"

To every rebuttal (I call them "yes, buts") that comes up in your mind, write down a counter affirmation and say it every day. Acknowledge small steps every day that you have taken towards reaching those goals.

Tell someone else what they are, so you stay accountable. Start small and build every day. You are on your way to making an internal shift that will then show up externally, and yes, picking one thing can make a change in many areas of your life.

Now go back to your list, and circle your top 3.

Ask, why do you want these?

If it was for someone else, like mine was, it probably won't have much staying power.

The big question is, who do you want to please? While wanting to make others happy is admirable, if it is at the cost of listening to your own heart and deferring your own happiness for someone else's, this can be detrimental to your self-esteem and health. While we often hear "the gift is in the giving," we can only do this when our cup is full.

If you don't have weight behind your want, it won't be compelling enough to achieve, or you might get it, but you won't be able to sustain it.

Take losing weight, for example. Only 20 percent of the people that lose weight are able to maintain their weight loss, and I would venture to say that it is because their *why* isn't big enough. Sure, heredity factors into this, and I would be remiss to not mention that, as a Fitness Coach, but habits contribute enormously to outcome. Your motivation must be big enough to sustain you through the tough times and temptations, or it won't have any staying power.

Oftentimes, I hear people say, "I want to lose weight or get in shape for a trip I am going on," but generally this either doesn't work, or they may lose weight for the trip, only to gain it back right after they return. Now, if you are losing weight or gaining weight for a movie you plan to be in, that is a different story, but for most of us, we just contribute to decreasing our ability to lose weight and keep it off with yo-yo dieting and following the latest fads.

In this case, it's important to keep probing at your *why*, and sometimes it takes hitting rock bottom in order to find it, or getting so "fed-up" with yourself that you finally have the impetus to do something about it.

Sometimes it takes a major catastrophe or health issue for people to wake up. Having a heart attack, being diagnosed with diabetes, etc. Getting to the root cause is imperative to getting the results you want, because it is the fuel you need to harness your power when things get tough, and you could kill for a bar of chocolate.

If you can't get to your *why*, ask yourself more questions:

How will this change your life?

Say in the example of weight loss, you are having back or knee pain. Less pressure on joints will result in less pain. You will also be able to enjoy simple pleasures like getting out of a chair, getting on the floor to play with your grandkids, or being able to have the stamina to keep up with them!

Make sure your *Why* is Big!

Sometimes, you must look at underlying causes when you keep saying you want something, but come up short and can't achieve it. For example, one of the things for me is that I'm always late, and it can be truly annoying for clients, family members and friends. I know it. I would like to change, I have tried to change, and I have even looked at the underlying cause and examined it. I remember waiting for my dad to show up to pick me up, and him either forgetting me, or taking hours to arrive. It kicks up abandonment issues that are so painful for me that I'd rather make someone else wait for me than be the one who must wait and experience these feelings. Even though I know this cognitively, I can do well for a while and then go right back to my old ways. My consequences probably would have to be huge, like the threat of losing my job, in order to change it. What it tells me is that I most likely must go back to those old times and really relive them to let go of them, something I avoid at all costs. And even though I'm a grown adult woman, the past still lingers deep inside. Some of you are shaking your head, "is she crazy, just do it!" and others can feel the pain of my words that hit you directly in your heart as you feel it and know what I am talking about. I am working on it, however, and can happily report I'm getting better. I've also built in a policy that says if I am traveling to you, I will be between 15-20 minutes late.

Now take each one of your top 3 goals and write down what your *why* is. You can always come back to the others later, but for now we will start here.

Goal:

Why I want this:

Goal:

Why I want this:

Goal:

Why I want this:

We will look at these in depth in the next chapter, but first I have something important to discuss...

Staying Present

The reason staying present to what *is* is so important is so we can stay open to the tiny voice inside ourselves that knows exactly what is right for us. So many times, when I am doing a life coaching session, people will say, "I don't know." They are so used to being told what to do, or thinking someone outside them has an answer to their problem, that they have lost their internal compass. We are fed this through advertising, big pharma, friends, family and professionals.

Being led to the right professionals, who can hear your concerns and help you navigate the best plan of attack for you, is critical. When we have eye issues, we go to the ophthalmologist; feet issues, the podiatrist; sports injuries, a physical therapist: you get the idea. But so often, we think someone else has the magic pill to help with our issues, and stop looking inside ourselves. The answers are always there if we are quiet enough to listen to the message trying to make its way to us.

Creation comes forth when we are still and quiet enough to hear the answers.

Sometimes, in a session, I might have someone write all of the pros and cons to their situation on each side of the page and then rip it up. Rarely are choices made based on what appears to make sense. There are steps, yes, but often the answers well up out of the quiet moments, giving space to birth the answer. Sometimes, when someone is stuck in their head thinking, evaluating and judging, I may have them stand and jump around, or we turn the music on and dance, and then stop abruptly as the answers sometimes jump up and out of them. Sometimes it is a case of sitting and waiting. The main thing here is to stop thinking that someone outside of ourselves has the answers.

When we stay present to what *is* instead of what *isn't*, we are able to connect with moment-to-moment truths that arise out of nothing. We are living and moving organisms, and life's magical moments happen when we stay out of our head, and remain in our hearts, where light bulb moments of certainty arise.

I have four children, three of whom were born at home. I wanted a home birth, but my husband wasn't comfortable with the first baby being born at home, so we agreed that I would birth at home for as long as possible, and if I had other children, they would be born at home. After a long, arduous back labor (my daughter was sunny-side up and literally pushing against my lower back). The doctor finally said, "we have to do something, this has gone on too long." I burst into tears, and sobbed for about 10 minutes. I was terrified of hospitals. I'm not certain why, but I was. Perhaps it was because I saw my brother in and out of them so often that I was afraid the same thing would happen to me. As they were reading all of the information about the epidural to get my consent, I thought, "if you're going to do this, *just do it* like Nike says" but I sat quiet, and in the next moment, I turned to the doctor and staff and said, "Stop, the baby's here!" They all looked at me like I was crazy, and came and checked. I went from four to ten centimeters dilated in ten minutes and was now ready to push. I pushed my 6 lb, 6-oz beautiful baby girl out within the next two hours.

I have taught pre-postnatal exercise classes and labor coaching, and attended quite a few births as a support person for the mother and partner. Some couples had other people with them, and at times decided they wanted them to leave, so I would help facilitate that. There are very little subtleties that affect the mother during labor, and energy in the room makes all of the difference. I'll never know if my labor would have gone quicker if I had stayed home, where I was comfortable, but I tend to think so.

My next 3 babies were born at home with a midwife. As a matter of fact, my midwife ended up not being able to come to my last birth, so I had to have the midwife that assisted her in my previous 2 births. She was an ophthalmologist and surgeon prior to being a midwife, and was very competent and kind, but, I just didn't connect with her the same way I had with my previous midwife. I was in light labor for only about 9 hours, and then I could feel it coming on fast and furious, and I really didn't want her to catch the baby.

I said to my husband, "go get the sheets warm, you need to catch the baby." With that, he called our dear friend, Susan, who had been at all of our other births, and said, "Susan, you need to come over, Cindy's having the baby" to which she replied, "ok I'll jump in the shower, and I'll be right over." He called her back immediately and said, "skip the shower, I need you here now."

When she walked in, I stood up and gave her a hug, and said, "I know you didn't plan on this, but I need you to catch the baby" (I had been holding her in). By now, the midwife had been called as well, of course.

With that, I squatted at the bedside, and pushed out another beautiful baby girl. Susan caught her first birth ever after being a doula at many home and hospital births. It was one of the most magical moments of our lives. The midwife arrived just in time to stitch me from tearing (I always tore) with her fine-tuned hands, as only a skilled surgeon could.

I tell you this story, not because I think anyone should or shouldn't have a home birth, but more to illustrate the aspect of staying in the moment. Birthing is one of those times when we are called right to the present moment, and if we can stay present to whatever is happening, things shift and change at a moment's notice.

When we embrace each breath, each moment as it arises, we can give birth to what is demanding to be expressed through us, not what our minds *thinks* is right.

We set our intention of what we want, ask the universe to support us, and listen intently. Then we act on what comes through us, and that is the magic. There is nothing being done to us to make things happen, but rather, we allow and trust that what is supposed to happen, will happen. Having people who can truly listen and hear you, and be there with you to give safe passage through the journey, is a critical component of outcome.

All of the exercises we have done in meditation, walking, singing, playing music, dancing, doing tai chi, yoga or exercising, being in nature, etc. are just inroads to stay in the present moment and open to its gifts. Life is *not* a dress rehearsal, and *no one* has the answers for you, but I promise they will arise as you stay open and present, which is the gift of your daily practice. But guess what? You have to do it for yourself!

Beneath the surface
goldmines hold secret treasures
deep within ourselves

Step 4: Plan of Action—Reaching Your Goals

Now it's time to get down to brass tacks and put your plan into action. You've seen it, you've dreamt it, and now you are excited to fuel your desire into tangible attainable goals, and launch forward. Congratulations on getting this far. Being clear and taking the time to define your goals puts you in the driver seat, enabling you to propel yourself forward towards success.

I will caution you from the outset that it might look daunting, impossible, and you may feel you don't have the skills necessary to reach your goals. Might I remind you of the words of Walt Disney: "The way to get started is to quit talking and begin doing"

My saying is always, "someone is going to win, and it might as well be you." If we let fear have its way, it will win every time. Don't worry, we'll get to how to deal with that later, but for now, it's time to make that all-important plan to help you actualize your dream. I just want you to know you are not alone if you find yourself thinking things like, "who do I think I am?" "I don't have the skills for that," "I am not smart enough," "I came from the other side of the tracks," etc. Some will give up, but not you, because you have made it this far in the book, so Kudos to you! You would have stopped reading a long time ago if you didn't have it in you to succeed.

Just know that every time you hear these self-defeating phases in your head, this is normal. The mind is doing a great job analyzing, judging, trying to keep you out of the fire: protecting you and keeping you safe. But it is limited in staying present and in the 'now,' so we must give it a little help in taking a backseat. Most often, when I hear these negative, critical voices now, I have learned not to give them any power. I laugh, acknowledge them and move forward, in spite of their self-limiting messages. When we don't give power to them, we can continue our plan of action.

If you're not there yet, don't worry: that's why you're here reading this book, and you will have a much better grasp on how to deal with the mind as we get further along the path. It takes practice reigning in this beast, much like little children in the playground, but with practice, it gets easier. It is our job to be patient and persistent while we learn a new way of being with ourselves in the world.

Life is a journey to be explored: take risks, feel the wind beneath your wings, change course, live the life you imagined, and feel the blessings that life has to offer you each day. Too often, we have bought into negative self-talk that cripples us and keeps us stuck, but with the right tools in your toolbox, you will soar, turning your dreams into reality.

For now, I just want you to befriend the beast, or at least

bear with it if you meet it along the way, and just know that this self-doubt is normal.

In the words of Hunter S. Thompson, "Life should not be a journey to the grave with the intention of arriving safely in a pretty and well-preserved body, but rather to skid in broadside in a cloud of smoke, thoroughly used up, totally worn out, and loudly proclaiming 'Wow! What a Ride!'"

Are you ready to bring those dreams to fruition? Good! Then pull out your pen or pencil again, or get your fingers tapping, while we write your action plan. You can write here below, or in your notebook or on your computer, whatever works best for you.

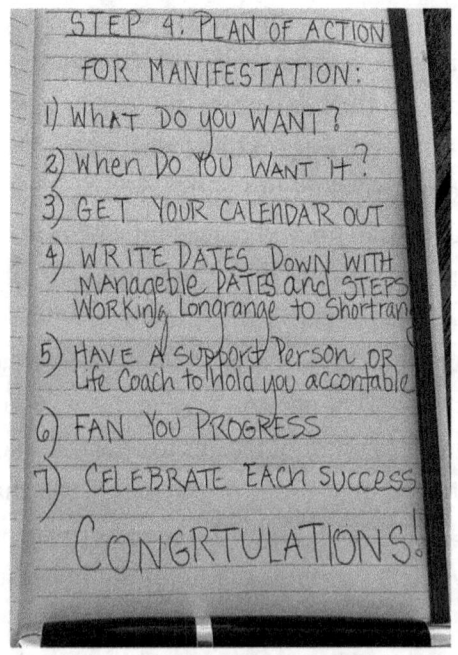

As you work through the plan, do the following:

1. **Write down all of the voices in your head when you think of launching your goal. That's right, the good, bad and the ugly.**

2. **What do you think will happen if you achieve what you say you want?**

3. **Will it make you happier, more successful, will people finally notice you, get you more money?**

4. **Who is this for? By now, I hope it was for you: but it's good to make sure.**

5. **What kind of support do you need?**

6. **I'll be happy when…?**

We often think that if we attain something, we will be happy. This is not always the case. For example, when people lose weight, or get the car, house or job they always wanted, etc. they think that will make them happy. We think that having things equals happiness, when in fact, we are still left trying to climb the ladder to attain something: a feeling or state of Nirvana. Then we may find it was right under our nose all along. Because satisfaction, which I prefer over happiness, is a state of mind, and we are about as happy as we make up our minds out to be, as Abraham Lincoln put it.

I have this sign in one of my rooms that I love because it speaks to this sentiment:

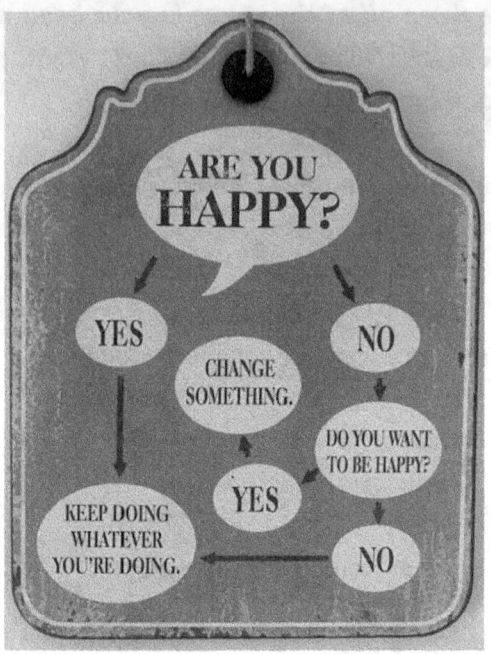

The fear of still being miserable even if we get our desired goal is often what keeps us from achieving it. As I write these words, I am very aware that this is my very first book, and might I let you in on another little secret? I'm terrified of writing it, and I really hate to share that with you because it makes me vulnerable, and makes me appear weak and fragile. What do I have to share that could possibly make a difference in your life? And yet I continue tapping away because I have always wanted to write a book and support people in achieving their dreams, much the same way I have come to achieve mine. I could scrap the book, but there is something inside that continues to want to be shared in the world, and as much as I try to ignore that, it continues to make its way known and asks to be written, so I continue.

If I look at the fears behind what is going on, I ask questions of myself in order to get inspiration. "Am I afraid it won't be good enough? Am I afraid to expose my vulnerabilities? Maybe no one will buy it, and I will be alone on the bookshelf and annexed before my time to shine." Even saying this out loud to you now, I feel small and little and hear the words of my father's voice: "Act as if;" "Never show your vulnerability;" "Get the upper edge;" "To show weakness is failure;" and I remember that I was taught that if I had false bravado, I could muscle my way through anything. I can, and I did, but that was just ego protecting me from my true self with all its beauty and its flaws.

When I tap into the Divine and drop the ego, life shows up for me, as it does for all of us, and it is there we can open to what the universe has in store.

I face the same fears as we all do in moving towards reach my goals. The only difference is, I've learned to keep going no matter what purple colored monster shows up on my doorstep.

Here's the truth, we never know what will happen until we achieve the goals we have set ourselves, and we will only get there by doing the work. One thing is for sure, and that is, we develop more trust in ourselves and the process when we do what we say we will do. That alone builds greater self-esteem. The other thing is, these are all lessons that are in our path to learn and grow from, and by not striving to achieve our goals, we stunt our growth and the ability to learn the intended lessons that create wholeness that we would have never known otherwise.

But if you never try, or start, you'll never know. Sometimes, we get so addicted to the negative voice in our mind, we become victims of what we've been told, and negative self-talk becomes habitual. There are many books on self-talk, but the crux of the matter is this: if you want a different outcome, you must change something. "The definition of 'insanity' is doing the same thing over and over again and expecting different results," as the famous saying goes.

Have I convinced you yet to *go for it?*

Now that we have cleared that path, let's look again at your first goal from Step 3…

Goal:

Date you want to achieve it:

Your "Why?":

Manageable incremental dates broken down (work backwards to forward):

What are the steps you must take to manifest the result you want?

How will you stay on track?

Who can you count on for support? Do you need to hire someone, or do you have friends you can ask?

What do you need from them?

What will throw you off?

What are your fears?

What will you do to get back on track?

Write down anything else that comes up:

Acknowledge your progress every day, and do something each day to move towards actualizing your goal. Make a copy of this chart, and check off your daily progress. You will have ups and downs, just know that, and jot them down as you go. It's important to fan your small successes and take things in bite-size pieces.

How You Start Your Day Matters

Do you hit the snooze button 3 times before you get up, drag yourself out of bed, run to the coffee machine, throw your clothes on, scramble for your keys, skip breakfast and then spill your coffee in the car? Are you frustrated and exhausted before you start your day?

Imagine for a minute, you wake up and take a minute or two to transition into your morning, while you stretch, taking a few deep breaths.

Then you move to the floor or a chair and spend as much time as you can in meditation, saying your daily affirmations, and stretching. You check your calendar, look at your 'To Do' list and prioritize (which you did before you went to bed as well). Remember, you probably won't get through it all, but it gets things out of your head. You make your coffee, eat breakfast, get dressed and then mindfully collect your keys that are always in the same spot. You get in your car relaxed, and feel peaceful.

We need time, and are deserving of it. Pushing ourselves aside and not listening to our internal cues sets up a negative spiral, circling like a merry-go-round, making it difficult to jump off and end this cycle. Notice the difference in how much more joyful and relaxed you feel, and how your interactions are so much more enjoyable when you give yourself time.

So yes, how you start your day matters! Try it and let me know how you feel.

Set yourself up for Success:

It is better to have a daily plan that you do the week before with your general priorities, and then schedule them into your week in order of importance.

Every night before you go to bed, look at what your schedule is to make sure you:

A) remember what you planned; and
B) check whether it still applies.

When you wake up in the morning, take another look at it to see if there are any adjustments you might need to apply.

Let me warn you, even in the best laid plans, there are problems which come up to throw your schedule out of kilter, and this can throw your whole day off of balance. Starting your day in this way puts you in front of the 8-ball, rather than behind it, and creates momentum to carry you forward.

Building a habit and having your daily plan: A blueprint for success

First off, let's aim for success right away. I don't know your work schedule, etc. Some of us work graveyard shifts and must accommodate for that, but it's still vital that you have a routine with some fundamental steps that will build good habits right away.

First, separate sleep from work. Keep your devices out of your sleeping space so you can get the rest you need to start the day refreshed. Check your room, and make sure it's conducive for sleep. If you need blackout shades, get them. If you need to take your television out of your room, do it. If you need a new bed, get it. If you wake up with ideas and must write them down so you can get back to sleep, keep a notebook and pen at your end table with a small light, and jot them down. Do not use your phone, or you're likely to see a text or email, or get hooked in in some other way.

Create your to-do list the night before, considering any appointments you have on the books.

1. **Start your day in meditation, breathing, stretching and setting your intention for the day.**

2. ***Check your daily schedule again. Make sure you haven't over scheduled, or perhaps you have already had an emergency you need to accommodate for.***
3. ***Make sure you are fueled and have scheduled self-care as well.***
4. ***Drink plenty of water to fire and fuel your brain.***
5. ***Set some mini goals for the day.***
6. ***Get up from your desk regularly and move, if you have a desk job. If you move all of the time, make sure you sit for a bit.***
7. ***Stop, look and listen to your internal needs when you get off track.***
8. ***Write down at least six things you are grateful for at the end of the day, and acknowledge yourself for that.***
9. ***Write down what you learned about yourself or your situation today.***
10. ***Plan your schedule for the next day.***

Congratulations… Now relax, and pat yourself on the back!

Note: You have to find what works for you. I have found this is the best formula for me. A top-selling author who I love, Kelly Notaras, who wrote *The Book You Were Born to Write,* chose to cut out her meditation while she was writing her book, which worked for her, but it would be truly disastrous for me. Meditating first thing in the morning sets the whole tone for my day, and truly helps me write and get to the things that are important for me to do.

Another hack I've learned is to couple something I don't

want to do with something I need to get done. For example, one way I've learned to take my vitamins is to get them out when my coffee is brewing and then take them with my first bite of breakfast. Make a list of all the things that you might try to couple to make things easier for you.

We all want the formula for living,
a step-by-step blueprint that tells us if we do this, this will happen.
For the most part it's true,
that if you make a plan and put it out in the universe, it will happen.

And yet life happens, as we know, when we're making other plans.
The real question becomes,
how do we keep our focus
while attending to what needs to be tended to?

Sometimes it's a dead stop,
and we have to change course, which can be shattering.
It throws us to the ground, tears us apart, and the life we envisioned is certainly not the one that we are living.

Anyone who has gone through a major trauma or episode in their lives, can tell us this.
Life is a sequence of mini earthquakes and aftershocks.

A rebuilding of our foundation and inner terrain.

I am in awe of those beating the odds of the unbeatable and finding a new direction, perhaps even better than the one they could ever have envisioned by accepting what *is* rather than mourning what *was*.

This is where the work comes in.

Let's take each one of these adversities into our hearts and prayers, that we might continue on our journey of listening to where we are, trusting what's happening, and never losing sight of where we want to go.

Dreams written in stone
carved steps pave the way towards
spiritual growth

Step 5: Loving Yourself

We are all love, at our deepest level, and until we love ourselves, we don't know what our purpose truly is.

It starts with you loving yourself, and then sharing that message of self-love with others who are ready to hear it. We are each worthy of love, and we need to break the barriers of separation and embrace our oneness, so we can make our planet a better place to be. We will always have "good and evil" in our world, but that doesn't mean we give up our mission and struggle. Quite the contrary, we need to be even more committed to our values and ideas. Leo Buscaglia was a professor in Los Angeles who wrote on love. He was born into an Italian family that loved to laugh, share and eat together. His mother always had a pot of polenta on the table, and sent him off to school smelling like garlic, but somehow, he didn't let the people who were poking fun at him upset him in any way. One of the things he is quoted as saying is, "Love always creates, it never destroys. In this lies man's only promise." And another quote that I've always loved of his is this:

"The easiest thing to be in the world is you. The most difficult thing to be is what other people want you to be. Don't let them put you in that position."

If you are sailing through, and all of the things you have put on your list are manifesting, congratulations. We all know those people who seem like anything they touch turns to gold, and they have very few barriers in achieving what they set out to do. Maybe that's you, but if you are like most of us, there will be some trials and tribulations to go through in order to bring your dreams to fruition. If you notice yourself being jealous, comparing yourself, feeling down in the dumps and having a lot of negative self-talk, it's time to investigate more.

I believe we all come into life with our own soul journey, a kind of roadmap with lessons we need to learn. Perhaps we have had many past lives we have had to progress through. If you're a skeptic like me and don't necessarily believe in past lives, it's ok. You will get your lessons either way. Some people know without a doubt that they have lived many lives before; others stumble on them by accident and when they do, a pathway opens up. Whether you believe in them or don't, what's important is to take some time to look at what is stopping you from getting what it is you say you want.

There can be many reasons, for example, the negative comments you've heard over the years, fear, doubt, not feeling worthy or good enough, fear of getting what you want.

Underneath all of that is loving ourselves. If we don't truly and genuinely love ourselves, it's difficult to create a path toward getting what we want.

If we heard positivity growing up, and learned how to deal with failure without attaching it to our self-worth, we have an easier road, no doubt, but even if you have not had that nurturing environment, and it wasn't safe to make mistakes, you can still learn how to nurture yourself. It's just going to take reframing and practice to get there. The good news is that it can be done. When we have been raised to embrace our challenges and learn from them, we are not held back by them.

Some people believe that life has given them a bad rap, and it's not fair. It isn't fair, but if you don't look beyond that, you will never have what you want. Blaming your past, and making others scapegoats, will never help you get what you want.

It's so easy to love ourselves when things are going well, which is often our ego talking, but when they are going badly, there is the opportunity to practice truly loving and accepting ourselves. This builds resilience and strength of character.

If you are sitting there and thinking, "but I've cheated; lied; am an alcoholic; drug addict; sex addict; gamer; have bipolar or schizophrenia; bulimia; anorexia; am obese; wheelchair-bound; have OCD; anxiety, or am depressive," the list can go on and on. This is all the more reason to love yourself, and get the help you need.

The first step towards loving yourself is to become aware

of what you are saying to yourself about why you can't love yourself. Start right there.

Each of us will have a different path to getting there, but it can be done, with the right support.

The bottom line is, no matter what, you are loveable and deserving of having what you want, no matter what you have been told. If you have done things you don't feel good about, it's important to make those right and make amends, so you don't keep repeating the same mistakes over and over. If you don't, just remember you will keep making the same mistakes until you get the lesson and don't need to repeat it anymore. The words of Dr. Cherie ring forever in my ear: "Love Yourself, Trust Your Choices And Everything is possible."

"So, how do you love yourself if you don't?" You ask.

Great question!

First, you must get to the root cause.

Get that pen out:

1. When is the first time you didn't feel loved?

2. **What happened?**

3. **What was said?**

4. **What decision did you make about yourself?**

5. **How do you change the pendulum? In other words, what do you need to do every day to love yourself?**

Let me just say that we are all deserving of love, and to be cared for and adored. Even if you think you are not worthy of love because you have done something you deem unlovable, it's important you forgive yourself for whatever it is you did or think you did that you are blaming yourself for, etc. Let it go.

In our pure essence, we are all love, and we don't have to do anything to prove ourselves worthy. Perhaps you have had to live up to standards of your family or society to receive accolades and love, but those are the constraints others have put on us, that have nothing to do with love.

Just as the sun is the sun, the moon is the moon, you are love. "But," you say, "I get angry, I'm sad, I've done stupid things, have not lived up to the standards to deserve love!" You are still love.

Just because we can't see the sun, it is still there.

People get confused when they feel feelings that are everything other than loving, thinking that they are bad people. *No!* We all have feelings of sadness, grief, apathy, loneliness, boredom and anger, but those are only feelings. We are not our feelings, and we cannot separate out our feelings any more than we can separate from love. Underneath all of that, we are love.

The problem is, we have learned to associate having bad feelings with being evil, or something other than love. That is simply not true. Everyone has feelings. The degree to which we are accepting of them, and know that they are not us, is the degree to which we can see our true essence.

Our true essence shines with light and love, and just *is*.

The problem is, we let our mind control us by judging our every move. The job of the mind is to criticize, compare, evaluate and try to fix things rather than to just *be*.

Our mind is not who we are, and when we know that, it doesn't have to control us. It tells us *we can't do that; we aren't good enough,* which is deadly, and keeps the vicious cycle going.

Our mind is great for figuring out a math problem, getting directions, etc., but not for teaching us how to love ourselves.

We need to access that deep place within that is pure light, joy, love: the place where we don't have to prove ourselves or do anything other than simply *be*.

So, first things first:

1. **Identify that you are being hard on yourself, or don't love yourself.**

2. **Realize this is your mind, not who you are.**

3. **Is it an old trigger? Where did you first hear this?**

4. **Forgive yourself.**

5. **Do what you need to do to be gentle and self-accepting. Forgive yourself.**

6. **Make amends if you need to. Apologize to yourself or others.**

7. **Stop and take a few deep breaths to access that deeper part of yourself to your essence.**

8. **Meditate, exercise, play music: anything to quiet the mind.**

Stop, Look and Listen

Here is a shortcut I like to use, because I remember hearing this in school and it is ingrained:

1. **Stop:** Stop whatever you are doing

2. **Look:** Look inside and see if this triggered a reaction from the past or a recent experience. If not, look at what's happening around you. Is someone intruding on your space? Is it noisy? Did you have an argument? etc.

3. **Listen** to your messages.

You need to be patient and kind to yourself and *stop all* beat-up.

Comparisons are the Kiss of Death

One theme I find with clients is that they often downplay their obstacles, and compare themselves to others, thinking they shouldn't be complaining when they have an amazing life. While they might want for nothing, and have all of the riches in the world, they still have deep-seated issues that gnaw at them and erode their self-esteem and ability to enjoy life to its fullest. Whether they struggle emotionally or physically, these are real everyday nuisances that are stopping them from enjoying what they have, and they are trapped in obsessive thinking and worry, and possibly also physical agony.

They feel guilty that they even have the audacity to complain with such a privileged life, and yet they suffer daily. You can have every material item known to man, and still be miserable. It's critical to stop that comparison of ourselves and self-judgement, because it keeps us from facing what is going on internally, and getting to the root cause. None of us make it out without obstacles: it's as simple as that, no matter who we are.

As the story goes, we can't pretend to know what someone is going through, unless we have walked in their shoes, and although they might look shiny and beautiful on the outside, shoes which don't fit are excruciating. So, remember the old saying, and don't judge a book by its cover.

Our feelings are trying to teach us something if we can just get outside of our thinking patterns and listen to the underlying message. We need to address these issues the same way we do with setting an objective, and be kind to ourselves. We begin by making it an objective to stop the self-judgement and self-sabotage. Often, we are afraid we will never be able to realise our dreams because of this internal suffering, but it's just not true. We need to remove the smokescreen in order to see what it is protecting us from. Sometimes deeper psychoanalysis and other forms of treatment can help eradicate these fears that are actually our friends, for they are trying to teach us something.

When Don Miquel Ruiz says in his book *The Four Agreements* not to take things personally, he is spot on. How many times do we think when someone hasn't called us back or done something they said they would do, that we did something wrong, and it's our problem?

Most often it has nothing to do with us! People have lives, they get sick, they have obligations, children and family. Sometimes they are in fact cleaning house and have decided to pull back and stop the relationship or friendship, but it doesn't mean we did something wrong. It has more to do with where they are in their lives. So, stop being so hurt and egotistical, which is what it really is, thinking it is about you. 90 percent of the time, it has nothing to do with you. So, treat yourself well and do what you need to do to love yourself.

The sum of all parts
both broken and beautiful
deserving of love

Step 6: Processing Feelings

So, you're on your way to reaching your goals: Congratulations! Often when we first start out on our steps, there is a clear path, and we sail through and have some momentum for a bit of time. It's sort of like a new love. Everything is rose colored. You are euphoric, and things flow easily and effortlessly, until you notice a flaw, or something happens that scares you and you react, or get triggered. If you're wise, you'll stop to see what just happened, and chat about it with your new love. By the way, finding a life partner might have been your goal. If you don't examine what just happened, you will start pulling away, making up stories, and perhaps end the relationship before it even has a chance because it is too painful to feel the feelings that came up.

Or, say you are embarking on starting a new business, have done a business plan, settled on a strategic plan of action, gotten funding and the deal falls through: what then?

This can derail you if you aren't careful, and you can stop dead in your tracks. Sometimes, that's the exact right thing to do, but it's important to stop and see what came up internally for you that you decided so quickly to abandon your efforts when an obstacle came up.

Old triggers of emotion, pain, anger, trauma, etc. get in the way of manifesting our dreams if we suppress them.

When we've had bad experiences in life, we don't want to go back to them. If you've ever touched a hot stove, you know the feeling of wanting to run and flee as far away from those feelings as possible. When in actuality, we need to run towards them and give them space to heal whatever next layer is coming up.

Of course, run from the fire if possible! Sometimes we don't have a choice, as we see in the courage of those in war, standing in the face of the enemy against all odds.

When we can experience what the feelings are trying to teach us, we can clear the debris from our path, and move forward towards our dreams.

As the world literally turns on its axis in unfathomable ways, we are all processing our feelings in many ways, shattered, in shock, and trying our best to stay afloat.

This is where having a life coach to ask you some pertinent questions comes in to help get you back on track and process the fears, so they don't get in the way of you attaining your goal.

Set sail towards your aspirations, and enjoy the process. Watch how doors and windows open up just by putting your desires out into the universe.

There is a magnetic force that aligns with your goals, and you may get unexpected phone calls, or new people that come out of the woodwork to support you.

When you start saying "yes" to yourself, and believe you are worthy of having what you want, doors open as if by magic. A lot of this is simply because you said "yes," stayed open, and got yourself out of the way, so the work can be done through you. Our crown chakra houses the universal connection with the Divine, and requires little from us but trust. There is no effort and work, only flow. These are principles open to everyone, not just a few select people. We are all capable of achieving our goals and dreams.

When we come to obstacles, these can bring up feelings of inadequacy, and it's important to recognize that. We are often triggered back to another time in our life without realizing it, and we can't move past that old wound until it is cleaned out and tended to.

Time to get back to the drawing board and get your pen out:

Ask yourself if this reminds you of another time?

What happened?

What were you feeling?

What were you afraid of?

What decision did you make about what happened?

What needs to be done to clear it up?

Often, we are operating from a time in the past, and this continues to show up in other ways. We find that until we make peace with whatever it was that happened, we can't move forward.

This can be a lot to unpack, but until we do, we will keep coming up to the same obstacle.

You will get a hint of what needs to happen so you can heal from that incident. It may come as a message to call someone and have a conversation, or feel the feelings you had at the time, but didn't want to feel. Often just feeling the feelings and realizing how hurt you were is enough to let go of hurt, pain and resentment so you can move on.

We stop ourselves from moving forward when we say, "I can't do that" and then we never try.

Say your goal is weight loss, and you have been doing great and have lost 20 lbs. You are feeling great in your clothes, you are healthier, stronger, have more stamina and are loving the way you look, and you still have 10 to go to get to your optimum weight. Then you eat something that sets you on an eating binge, and you can't control yourself. What do you do then? How do you get back on track?

If you beat yourself up, you can continue to perpetuate this whole cycle, and gain the weight back, unless you stop yourself right then and there and get to what is going on underneath the surface.

Once you've identified the problem, that's half the battle to resolve it and get back on track.

Imagine being born into a world where someone looked into your eyes and saw through to your divinity, and there was no proving ground needed to be who you are.

We learned lessons from our environment by touching a hot stove and pulling back, dodging a car in the middle of the street, or surviving a skinned knee, but we were never chastised by failure.

We learned what we had to do to fit in in the world and, in some instances, were told what we had to do in our lives career-wise, who we had to marry, etc. to be successful. This can create tension and dis-ease when we do not fit someone else's expectations of what someone wants for us: namely our parents or colleagues, and we are constantly aware of not measuring up.

There is a schism in our psyche, because we want to please, yet we might have a different idea of what we want. There is a lot of pressure growing up to get good grades, fit in, be popular, be polite, etc., and we may have never really looked at what that cost us, or how we felt about it. Consequently, we may harbor resentment that we are not even aware is there. Maybe we were forced to play piano or be on a sports team when that was the last thing we wanted to do, but couldn't communicate that, so we repressed those feelings in order to please others. These feelings often come up when we are in progress towards one of our goals. Rather than push them away, it's important to bring them to the light and examine what those feelings are, so they don't hinder your progress in the future.

It can be difficult, because if we weren't raised to have our own minds that fostered independence, we can feel as though we will never amount to anything unless we do what is expected of us, and ignore our inner yearnings.

We often live out someone else's dream for them, instead of finding out what makes our heart sing; we are programmed by other's wishes, never knowing we might have another choice. When we don't fit the mold someone has set for us, we can be shamed into being someone we aren't, which is where problems come in, and we can never discover our true nature and life's purpose. Clearing out the debris is the first step of ending trauma and allowing your essence to shine forth.

Remember, processing feelings is the inroad to the soul, and by clearing the debris you are opening a pathway to reaching your goals and living the life you envisioned.

Sometimes stopping and hiring a life coach or a therapist is essential so you can get to the root cause and let go of these debilitating obstacles that block your success. Or sometimes you need both. The way to figure that out is, if there are deep underlying issues that aren't clearing up with life coaching, and the lightbulb doesn't go on, you know you there is some kind of pain, PTSD or some other form of mental health issue that is preventing you from actualizing your goals, and until this is cleared up, you are paralyzed.

Other times, body work such as Craniosacral Therapy, Reiki, Yoga, Qigong, Tai Chi Shamanic Healing, Chakra Cleansing, Acupuncture, etc. can release emotional and physical pain stored in tissue, and once it is released, you are back on your way towards achieving your dreams.

Mind, Body and Spirit

As a life fitness coach, I deal with the body, mind and spirit, which sounds so cliché, but it's true. The reasons I do so many modalities in my work are twofold. Many of my certifications were driven by instructors who didn't show up to teach. When my obstetrical nurse/midwife from USF in San Francisco didn't show several times, I got certified in pre- and postpartum exercise, baby massage, and birth coaching.

At the end of personal training sessions, I would stretch clients, and they would ask me to come back and do massage because, they said, "you have the best hands." It was the last thing I wanted to do, but with loyal clients, I got certified and now have countless hours in training in many modalities, including craniosacral therapy, soft tissue mobilization, etc. It actually gives me more insight into what is going on with the body, so I can help on many levels. Being a Reiki master (which is simply energy work and hands-on healing using symbols of the ancient teaching, both in drawing or visualization) allows channels to release and open. Each modality has its gifts, and each person is unique, and processes things differently, so it's important to have a lot of tools in your tool chest.

When a friend/client wouldn't take "no" for an answer, and wanted me to teach her private spinning class, I balked, and flat out said "no, I hate spinning." She was persistent, and when this friend talks, people listen. She made me a deal I couldn't refuse, and we flew the friendly skies to the big island of Hawaii, where I worked privately with the spin teacher who trained me.

I loved the camaraderie of the girls, and it was a great workout, but with six hens that were good friends, chatting, with some vying to take over and teach, it wasn't working, and she finally hired a "real" spin teacher who was hardcore, and loved spinning. Thankfully, I retired from this venture, although my bruised ego and pocketbook took a hit, and it took time to adjust. The same friend continues to support my endeavors, whatever I decide to do, for which I am eternally grateful.

I tell you these stories for two reasons:

One, so you can remember that life continues to lead us on the next stage of our journey, if we listen to where we are being called, and say "yes," even if we are nervous and scared. We may feel like we are in a rut, but we should ask, are we listening and staying open to whatever gifts come our way? I've also learned that saying "no" when you don't know, or when you're not sure, is vital as well. When we stay open and optimistic, we are malleable, soft and adaptable. When we become rigid and hold on to our pain like a badge of courage, we become stiff and brittle.

Two, because the body and the mind are intertwined, and each one speaks to the other both physically and metaphorically. Pain shows up in our body as symptoms, and often times these symptoms mirror how we are living our lives. Each body part that has a particular issue is related to an emotion that can be stored in our body. There are charts on energy work which you can use to see at how they are affecting you, but your insight about what is going on in your own body is the best teacher.

I was working with a client in a life coaching session once who wanted to quit smoking. Prior to that, I had been training her, and I told her that by the time she was 60, she had to quit, and best to do it sooner than later. We shifted over to training after the life coach session, and so many emotions would surface, as you might expect if you have ever battled such an addiction. Sometimes she would just stop and cry. Other times I gave her batakas to hit, or put punching gloves on her, and she would hit the punching bag, and we would do kick boxing. Luckily, she quit and never returned to smoking. She always had a cough that concerned me that wouldn't leave. About five years later, she went to the doctor for a check-up, and they discovered a small cancer spot on her lungs. It was such early-stage cancer that they were able to go into the side of her chest with a needle and remove one of her lungs through the needle. Because of her commitment to training, she has been a shining example, and her pulmonary doctor is highly impressed with her respiration. She is still hiking, and stays isolated when necessary to avoid colds, etc., but her life is a remarkable testament to living with purpose and listening to her body's messages.

We must also look at what we say to our bodies and make sure we are not creating dis-ease by repeating mantras that aren't helpful, and instead, replace these with positive affirmations.

Re-Framing

Take a few minutes to look at what you say to yourself constantly and see if you can reframe it in a positive way to create imagery that is productive and shifts the mind consciously. This works on your unconscious mind as well.

Balanced and peaceful
waterfall clears minds unrest
refreshed by torrents

Step 7: Falling off the Wagon, Burnout & Support

Whatever your goal is, there will be times when you fall off the wagon, so to speak, and fall short of what you want to achieve. Perhaps something will set you back. It happens sometimes. Say you have been losing weight and are happy with how you have been looking, then you go off course and gain a couple of pounds. The sooner you can catch yourself and get back on track, the better.

The problem with most people is that they feel bad and start cycling backwards, letting some of their habits slip and returning to the ways that didn't serve them. This is where the work comes in. Stop yourself right then and there and ask questions to work out what derailed you in the first place. This is precisely how I learned to get to my goal weight and stay there once and for all without yo-yo dieting ever again. It's also how I have been able to tackle each objective I want to have in my life, and take action to create long-lasting results. The proof is in the pudding, so to speak. Desire + Commitment = RESULTS.

You might wonder, 'how can I be happy, see the light, and find joy, when all I see is the dark and anxiety that lurks within?' You try so hard. You eat all the right foods, meditate, read, go to classes, take your vitamins, exercise and still there is a hole, filled with looming doom.

Go to your cave and sit. "But." you say, "I can't possibly do that, it will catch me, and I will wither and wilt, and perhaps I'll go mad!" Will you? Have you ever really stopped running? Take each moment as it is, and breathe. When we think there is something wrong with us, any feelings of darkness grab us by the throat and grip harder until we're gasping for air. Jack Kornfield, mindfulness meditation teacher and author says "Being on a spiritual path does not prevent you from facing times of darkness. But it teaches you how to use the darkness as a tool to grow."

You are not your feelings, your thoughts, or your mind. Your mind is just doing its job to keep you in this constant prison of doom and gloom. When we see this truth and don't give it power, we become free.

Sometimes we fall, we stand up, brush ourselves off, and are back in no time at all. Other times, we hit the edge head on, and we don't get up for quite a while. Of course, it feels much better when we can shake things off and move forward, but perhaps the fall wasn't enough to get our attention, and we find ourselves in the same position again and again, until we finally get the message the universe is trying to deliver.

Hopefully we stop for a moment and see where we might

need to slow down, pay attention, maybe buy a pair of glasses, or make some adjustments in our lives. If we hit that sharp edge, and we come face-to-face with life and can't get up, it takes an enormous act of courage, determination, support, steadfastness and due diligence to hang in there until we can move again.

These things that bring us to our knees in pain, tears, and suffering can feel like arrows going straight through the heart, both physically and emotionally. Nonetheless, the journey to finding peace often includes such trials.

I think of countless friends and clients who have walked this journey broken with heartache. Facing a lifetime of torment, yet continuing to get up again. On the outside, it may not look like someone knows this path, however, you can never be certain. I've been to hell and back, and I don't want to go there again. No matter what you're facing, how abandoned, neglected, angry, or afraid you feel, remember the same rule applies when you fall: put one foot in front of the other. The sun will set again, the moon will rise, the flowers will bloom, and you will get up again, no matter how badly you may have been bruised. I have seen countless people prove this, time and again, and I am in awe of their courage and bravery, and honored to be a witness to it. This includes witnessing my own progress.

IT'S NOT EASY, BUT IT IS POSSIBLE!

When I walked into the massage room one day, one of my clients was already laying on the table, as instructed by the sign outside that asked, "Please enter changed." Although I've had that sign on the door for as long as I can remember, my client who had also been on the table countless times was the first person who ever looked at the sign and read it from the vantage point of internal changing. She's going through profound shifts in her life, discovering herself for the first time, and considering her needs. No wonder it had this impact on her.

What if we saw that sign in our head daily, and we contemplated what it would look like for us to show up differently to create a different inner reality? There are many signs like these that we are unable to see because we are on automatic pilot going through life.

Walk through your life today with new eyes. Slow down, look at what's in front of you, look at what's been there all along, and start noticing how your world reflects what you see. Sometimes it takes dramatic incidents to act as a wake-up call, for us to finally get these messages of truth. Forget how long it took you to get back on the trail, and just be grateful you are there.

If you break it down to the most fundamental steps to getting back on track, you can do it. It's not rocket science, and it's pretty easy once you get the hang of it. Once again, it's time to...

STOP: Stop, slow down, and catch yourself.
LOOK: Look at what got you off track, and consider what the lesson is.
LISTEN: Listen to your messages of how to get back on track, and implement them, now!

One of the biggest mistakes people make is to say, "I'll do it tomorrow: just one more day and then I'll start." The problem is, we will never start anything if we continue that pattern. We must break the pattern. This is a made-up illusion that someone told us, which is why we are always trying to get there, or get finished. Certainly, you have tasks to perform, and there are important steps you need to complete in order to attain your objective, but life happens moment to moment, and we need to learn to roll with the punches, stop and adjust to what is happening at this very moment.

Life is a continuous journey, and we always need to take ourselves into account as our world turns.

Dr. Chérie said to me, "Cindy, I think you need to write a Netflix movie, not a book" and I just looked at her in dismay at the time. Now I nod a knowing "Yes." Never say "Never." You see, I don't watch much news or TV, because the characters in my life are like a soap opera in and of themselves, and I have to be careful not to get thrown into the drama.

Recently, I felt like my life had suddenly moved into a place of biting off more than I could chew, and I felt overwhelmed. Wait, shouldn't the author of a book on creating the life of your dreams have all of the answers and not feel feelings of negativity, worry, concern, exhaustion, etc.? Not at all! We can't control life situations that happen around us. People in our world get sick, die, end up in the hospital, get married, divorce, have babies, etc. The only thing we *can* control is *ourself*.

If I let the things that are happening around me take over my psyche, I would never be able to get anything done. We recently finished phase 1 and 2 of our home remodel. Our daughter got married between one of the phases, and the welcome party was at our house. We lost my stepfather, my aunt died, my 97-year-old father-in-law fell and broke his hip, and, after a long hospital stay, we moved him out of retirement living to assisted living. My father is nearly legally blind with macular degeneration and glaucoma and is in a lot of physical pain. He has to rely on Ready Wheels to get him places, and lives with his 92-year-old girlfriend up the hill who just broke a vertabra in her spine. My dad had Mohs surgery for carcinoma and stayed with us for a week while I took care of him, my brother ended up in ICU with 3 TIAs, a blood transfusion, tumors on organs, had every test known to man, and became combative in the hospital as he suffers from a mental health disorder. My mother at 87 drives him to appointments, when she's not doing Healing Touch, volunteering her time, which is a gift to all she touches. I try to check in with both of my parents daily.

My daughter came home from her honeymoon and announced she was pregnant, which is exciting, and yet a lot to deal with, as I'm trying to finish my own baby, this book. Three weeks later, my other daughter announced she is pregnant, right behind her sister. She was told she couldn't get pregnant, and I told her I would help her look into freezing her eggs, but I certainly wasn't ready for it now. She is not married, and said, "I will need to move in with you for a while." My contractor's wife died unexpectedly at 60, and we need to finish phase 3 of the project before we can consider anyone moving in with us. We have things from my father-in-law's house everywhere, things from the remodel, new baby gear coming in after I just decorated and thought I had some time for some R & R. The physical and emotional drain has left me exhausted!

On top of this, I got sick, which I never do, but it's not surprising with my immune system no doubt low. Need I say more? Now you can understand how Chérie thought I should write a Neflix movie.

I include these details from my own life to illustrate the point that, life happens, regardless of our plans and aspirations. We cannot control the circumstances around us, but only our reactions to them.

First of all, it's important to give voice to our frustrations, exhaustion, upset, etc. and then we have to STOP, LOOK and LISTEN.

There is a tendency to think we don't have a choice, and move into overdrive to accommodate all of the things people need without checking in with ourselves. We may be tempted to walk down the beach and never return.

When I stop and ask:

How do I feel?
What do I want?
What are my boundaries?

I can put me back in the driver's seat of my life, and see what I want and I am willing or not willing to do. It's my life, right?

Here are my own answers to the questions above:

How I feel is exhausted, (did I say that already?) upset (I want my own time), scared, sad, (who knows what will happen?), put-upon, overwhelmed (I usually pick up the slack, but don't have the reserve right now).

What I want is some time to myself, a conversation about how and if it will work to have my daughter and a baby living here, and some kind of time frame and schedule if she does.

During all of this, a dear friend called and said, "my boyfriend can't get a passport, and I would love you to come on this Yoga/journal retreat with me." My first thought was "I can't leave in the midst of all of this" and yet, I had just thought if someone handed me a trip with all the details set, I would jump on the next plane. She said, "I have miles;

I'm upgrading you to first class, and you only have to pay for a fraction of the cost." The universe always hears and delivers our needs if we listen. If this isn't magic, I don't know what is.

So, I headed out to spend time in quiet meditation and reflection and left my amazing supportive husband in charge.

A lot could have happened when I was gone, and I might have needed to come home early, but with the support of others to check on things as well, I took this time for my own personal sanity. I also put in an intention with the gods that be, to take care of everyone for me.

And guess what? No one died when I was gone, (whew!) and they all lived just fine without me. When I returned, I was better at helping take care of everyone else for having taken some care of myself. I could think more clearly, having carved out a niche for myself and come back into balance, feeling more relaxed and peaceful.

The Sandwich Generation

Many of us live in the 'sandwich generation' today, with kids waiting longer to have their own kids, and with parents who are aging with increasing needs, which is challenging at best. Setting priorities becomes vital. It's important to realize we can't do everything, and say *no* while setting boundaries. It is no easy task so make sure you schedule time for *you* in your calendar every day, whether it be a walk, lunch, reading, sitting in nature, calling a friend, etc. Whatever gives you the sustenance you need to stay rejuvenated and refreshed.

Delegate, and get a team to support you so you don't have to do all the heavy lifting.

When we realize we do not need to pick up the pieces for others, we can choose what we want or don't want to do, this empowers us to honor ourselves, and encourages others to do the same for themselves, so it is a gift to both of us.

While this might sound selfish to some of you, as I boarded the plane and left, consider that it is impossible to care for others truly if we can't care for ourselves. If you felt it was selfish, most likely you need some time for yourself to put *you* front and center of *your* life.

This will more than likely be the only window of time for me to have gotten away before these babies bless the world with their presence, if we are lucky enough to have them.

You might have to take it a step further and ask more questions. If that's the case, get your pen and paper out and ask yourself these questions:

1. **What just happened?**
2. **What am I feeling?**
3. **What got me off track?**

4. *What fears are resurfacing?*
5. *What are the lessons?*
6. *Do I feel deserving? Why or why not?*
7. *What do I need to do to get back on track?*
8. *What have I gained from my progress?*
9. *Forgive yourself.*
10. *Recommit and start now!*

Break things down into manageable chunks, and notice how you feel when you are keeping your commitment with yourself.

There is something that grows inside as you start developing a trust within that you can count on yourself to do what you said you would do, and this feeds your soul internally.

Exercise, Exercise, Exercise!

If one of your goals was working out, notice how you feel when you do that. At first, you might be sore and tired, adjusting to your new routine. After a while, however, you begin to feel energized as endorphins kick in. You have that natural high, and begin to look forward to that feeling continuing to grow in your life.

When I'm working with someone that is just starting out on a fitness plan and is struggling to do it, sometimes all I need to do is tell them to put on their workout shoes every day. Then I might direct them to go outside to get their mail, then walk around the block, increase the next week to 2 blocks, and we keep building from there. If we are doing exercises, bands, free weights, yoga or pilates, the same principle applies. We start with a base program and add new exercises, increase weight, repetitions and tempo as the body develops, in order to avoid injuries and undue load on muscles and joints.

The three main components of having a sound exercise program are:

- **Cardiovascular health** for your heart
- **Strength training** for strong muscles and to hold your skeletal muscles in place
- **Flexibility and stretching** to keep you supple and elongated, keeping space between your spine and organs.

There are a lot of books out on this subject, which can give you the skinny on exactly how much is needed, but rules of thumb that I follow and teach are: walking 6 days for 30 min to an hour, strength training for about 45 minutes, and daily stretching for 20 min to 45 minutes.

Exercise rejuvenates you, and oxygenates your brain and body, giving you more energy to reach your goals. Sometimes it's tough, but 9 times out of 10 my clients are happy they pushed themselves to work out when they wanted to throw in the towel.

When we are trying to break unhealthy habits, it's important to find alternatives to give our minds and bodies a job to do while we create our new reality.

Many of us are so addicted to the pleasure center in our brain, we don't know how to defer gratification and succumb to that extra cookie, watching more TV than is good for us, or playing video games. The more we break that cycle, the sooner we will reach our objective. There are, however, times when we just burn out, if we aren't careful and catch it before it catches us.

Burnout:

Burnout is a real thing, and it happens when you are trying to burn the candle at both ends, biting off more than you can chew. When we forget we are human beings and become human *doings*, we forget that we need time to recharge our batteries, so we can regenerate and restore.

A clue that you are in burnout is when you are constantly doing and giving out, with nothing coming in. You can be sure that is burnout. While it's true that "the gift is in the giving". You have to have something coming back. It's important to regroup and build self-care into your day. Schedule time for yourself, detach from device usage, and give yourself a physical and mental vacation. We all need them.

Food as Medicine:

We are the best stewards of our body's health. It's important to remember that as long as we live there will be new diets that are actually old ones, couched as cutting-edge nutrition. While we continue to learn more about the human body and every aspect of the world around us, there are some basic truths about eating healthy that are tried and tested. Many of the diets we have heard about get shifted and changed to new names, but are the same old same old. The big buzz words today are "intermittent fasting." This might work for some bodies, but not all, and to maintain blood sugar levels, smaller meals throughout the day are helpful for many if that is an issue for you. My 12 Step program to a Slimmer You consists of listening to your body, eating when you're hungry, and stopping when you are satisfied, to get you to your optimal weight. It has worked really well for me and many others I have worked with over the years, and has helped them to get to their goal weight. There have been days when I have only eaten 1 or 2 meals a day and I've felt great, and my weight has been stable for years now. Many would term this as "intermittent fasting," however that isn't why I was doing it. I was simply listening to my hunger cues. Recently, I started feeling a little dizzy through the day, went back to smaller meals more frequently and am feeling much better. It's important to listen to the messages our body is giving us, and adapt and make changes. Our bodies let us know what they need if we stay attuned to our signals.

Sometimes, we have heredity factors that come into play, and often we can combat these through lifestyle changes. Some things are out of our control, however, and require specialists to assist us, so it's important to heed those messages. There are times we have done all the right things and we still get sick. Never blame yourself for things that are out of your control, and seek medical attention right away for these conditions.

However, it's important to do everything within your power to take good care of your body, as it truly is your temple.

The 3 key words when trying to live a healthy life are:

Prevention!
Prevention!
Prevention!

It is up to us to ensure we are taking good care of ourselves, and not relying on the medical system to make us well. Medical doctors are a godsend when we have a disease, but it is our job to prevent ourselves from getting sick in the first place if possible. We do this by following a healthy diet, exercising, managing our stress levels and staying hydrated (i.e. if you are 130 lb, you need to drink 65g of fluid a day).

I firmly believe eating real food, not processed foods with plenty fruits, vegetables, whole grains and lean proteins, and staying hydrated with good healthy fats is the best way to care for our bodies.

Ending Obsessions

Do you sit and perseverate about the same subject over and over in your mind, your head spinning like a top? Is it common for you to repeat past behaviors, and unproductive thoughts? Although whatever stimulus has ended, you are practically addicted to repeat or prolong an action, thought, or utterance.

Obsessions and addictions show up in many different forms. Whether it is alcohol, drugs, food, gambling, women, men, etc., they all are like a constant broken record that you play over and over in your head. For some recovered addicts, the desire for another drink, cigarette, girl, guy, might never leave, even though you have stayed away from your vices for years.

A few words of advice: If you've never gone down these paths, d*on't! Then you never have to worry about quitting.*

This is easier said than done, however. And, since you're reading this, chances are you are knee-deep down the tunnel.Let's dissect this further and see if you can make heads or tails out of what's going on. Ask yourself the following questions:

When did all of this start?

Who were you with?

What did it serve you back when you first started?

What were you looking for?

How were you feeling?

What were you hoping for?

When did you notice you were hooked?

What does it give you now?

Do you want to be a victim of your situation, or do you want to change?

What will it take to do that?

Ok, so I've thrown a lot of questions out without any answers, and you might say, "Hey, if I knew the answers, I wouldn't be in the situation I am now, or reading this book. Just tell me what to do!"

The problem is, I can't spoon-feed this to you, but trust me, I would if I could.

If you skimmed all those questions, do yourself a favor and go back and take some time answering each one, then write them out until you're done.

Continue adding to this list.

Chances are your answers came from a place of self-loathing, feeling inadequate, not good enough, and wanting to fit in.

Once you see that, you see what this addiction has been trying to protect you from.

The next step is asking, "Am I ready to let this go"?

If you're not, *stop reading!* It's ok. Maybe you never really want to change, but are content being a victim and blaming people all of your life, which gives your ego some satisfaction of being right. It's the booby prize, but so be it for now. Just remember that your addiction will never give you peace and joy. You obviously haven't hit rock bottom yet, so wait until you're ready to make a change once and for all.

When you are ready, continue here.

Ask what you really want, and write that out clearly, with steps to keep you on track when you want to fall back to your old ways.

Make a timeline and follow it, "I will do this for one day or one week," and keep remaking it.

Get a support network.

Hire a life coach, a therapist, get a buddy, join a group, and have an outlet of other things that fill you, so you can draw on this when you feel yourself sliding back.

In a nutshell, this addiction has taken over because it has its own mind.

We could go back into your history. Many times, it's important to see how you got to this point in the first place, but only to heal these parts of yourself, so you can move forward. Like a gardener removing weeds from their garden, continue to clear it out, until they're gone.

Addiction protects us from feeling painful, unwanted emotions. Running away from confronting these sentiments keeps us from sitting with ourselves long enough to heal. We allow ourselves to live in a vicious circle until we get tired from this craziness. The adrenaline rush of extreme high and excitement drives us to these places of euphoria, so we don't have to endure dreaded periods of despair and anxiety. The very thing we don't want to feel keeps us in constant flux and instability because we can't come face to face with ourselves.

Start cultivating your own interests, and find what they are. Discover what gives meaning to your life, and how do you ground yourself to get there? What activities, people, places and things give your life substance and joy?

What is your bliss without the addiction?

Is it hiking; playing tennis; meditation; yoga; surfing; golfing; dancing; going to the movies; bingo; bridge? Whatever it is, make it part of your daily routine.

Breathe, trust the process, and seek others that are committed to growth and change as well.

The Magic Bullet: Combating Fears and Phobia

There is a magic bullet, and the magic is *you* uncovering your beautiful, free self while you continue on your journey.

Remember: *"You are never given a wish without also being given the power to make it come true. You may have to work for it, however."*- Richard Bach

Remind yourself of that, and never lose hope, no matter

how hopeless or long the situation has been going on. While it might feel like forever, and as though it will never change, all of life is about change, and all things come to pass with time.

All the books, tapes, and lectures will *not* help you unless you actively do the work.

I wonder if the one-cup blender is so popular because we are all looking for the Magic Bullet in our lives.

The magic is there, hidden behind layers and layers of denial and unconsciousness. We must peel back the onion skin to get to the core of that truth, which takes time and patience.

We take a pill for everything these days, and hope it will take away all of our troubles, so we can be worry-free. I know a lot of people who take a pill for less than a hangnail. We are a quick-fix society, and we want to be happy, rich and skinny all the time. Who doesn't! With social media in our faces 24/7, seeing people sharing their happiest moments or what "looks" happy in a picture, it's easy to compare and judge our own life, discounting ourselves and thinking these people have the perfect lives. Reality gets left out of those pictures, and we don't see the morning face of wrinkles before makeup or a shave, taking out the garbage or sitting on the pot; thank God! But, nonetheless, we extract out of it, "Everyone is having an amazing life but me." It's the farthest thing from the truth.

You will hear people who have found something that has worked for them as if by magic, and that is awesome. Staying open to trying new things which bring hope and change is something which we never want to lose sight of, but it is generally learning to hold yourself through the ups and downs and surrounding yourself with a network of support that penetrates through to the magic inside you.

As we grow and move forward into the light and find solutions to problems, we continue to unfold and bring more joy to our internal world.

For some, meditation is vital, and needs to be adhered to, together with a self-care routine of exercise, affirmations, a healthy diet, sunshine, family and friends, in order to fully thrive. I wear a tee shirt that says "Fully Meditated" to remind me to clear my mind, and it works most of the time. When someone suffers with a phobia, or something that is debilitating, creating anxiety, darkness, panic and immobility; it is scary, and can lead to a vicious cycle which takes patience and to combat. Yes: It can feel like you are going into battle, and the battle ultimately is with yourself. If you have your armor and tool bag ready, you can beat this! I often say, "it's only your mind, and you are not your mind" but it is easier said than done to remember this, because the mind is so cunning and seductive: it will take us down if we don't catch it right away.

The job of the mind is to keep us in a state of judgment. Underlying your mind is your higher self that loves, supports and is nonjudgmental, and that is what we need to practice accessing until we master it. Because that is the place that sets us free, where peace and tranquility reside. When I was suffering from panic attacks, one of the most helpful things I did was lifting the heaviest weight I could lift to keep me in the present moment. I would feel the metal in my hands as I took deep breaths and counted. Counting gave my mind a job, and breathing cleared out the anxiety. As a result, I felt stronger and more in charge, and in time I felt calmer, as the anxiety released. Tai Chi, yoga, and walks had the same effect on me. It's important you find what works for you.

Stopping the beat-up cycle

It usually goes like this: the imagined fear is a thought in your head which provokes a feeling of panic, shakiness, doom and gloom, etc. Then the mind comes in that says, "oh no, here we go again," which sets an alarm off in your head, creating worry. When worry sets in, you move out of the present moment (which is what starts this vicious cycle) and further worry sets in about the upcoming event, which takes you out of the present moment where everything was fine. Fear takes on a life of its own. We start worrying that this is going to take us over, which sets up a chain reaction of 'fight or flight' in our bodies, sending out messages and chemicals which are released that shoot adrenaline racing through our bloodstream, exacerbating the problem of increasing cortisol levels. Depression sets in, because we then worry we will never get out of this cycle, and we feel powerless, hopeless and full of despair.

We must break the cycle. Sometimes medication is needed to help the synapses in the brain recover, so we can take advantage of doing the other things that feed us emotionally and get us back engaged in life, bringing us the peace that is rightfully ours.

Meditation, exercise, breathing, affirmations, eating and drinking healthily: it is imperative to do these every day in order to keep you in the present moment, and see what is driving you. There is always a trigger, and something that the fear is protecting you from on a deeper level.

When this happens to you, try this step-by-step action:

1. Identify the feeling
2. Ask what this feeling is trying to protect you from. There is always something.
3. Ask yourself what is the worst thing that can happen.

When your mind starts the vicious cycle of negativity, fret and worry:

1. STOP in your tracks
2. Breathe: Slow your breath and count 8 counts in, hold your breath 5 counts and then breathe out for 8 counts. Do this 8 times, or continue until you slow down enough and relax your mind and body.

3. *Look at what triggered the worry, and what it's trying to protect you from.*
4. *Have a list of affirmations that you can say to counteract each one, and say them to yourself silently or out loud until you feel a shift.*
5. *Circle white light of protection all around you and take a touchstone with you in your pocket.*
6. *Tell yourself, "Me and the fear are walking together, and I will be ok."*
7. *Have a list of things you can do when this happens that will soothe you and bring you back to calm and peace and serenity.*
8. *Stay in the present breath until you calm down.*

Example list:

1. *Meditate: Sit, light a candle, burn incense.*
2. *Breathe: Pick a flower and breathe in the scent. Deep breathing, breathing techniques with counting, or find other techniques. Go to yoga and learn. Growth breath work is great.*
3. *Remind yourself this is protecting you in a weird way, and you will be ok.*
4. *Go for a walk.*
5. *Call a friend.*
6. *Write in your journal.*
7. *Go to a movie.*
8. *Stay present in this moment only.*
9. *Say your affirmations.*
10. *Plant a plant.*

THE CYCLE OF BEAT UP

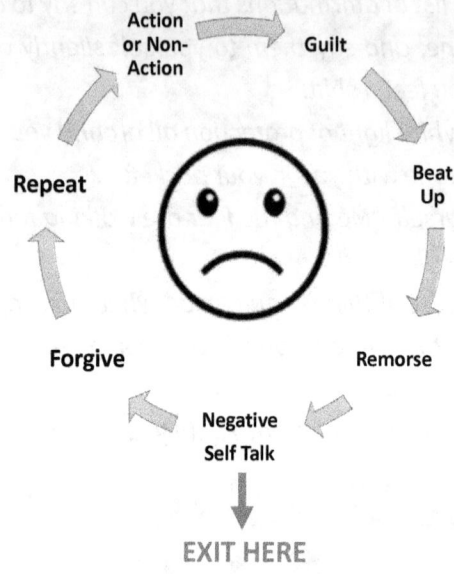

Break the Cycle ASAP
STOP – LOOK – LISTEN (to your messages)

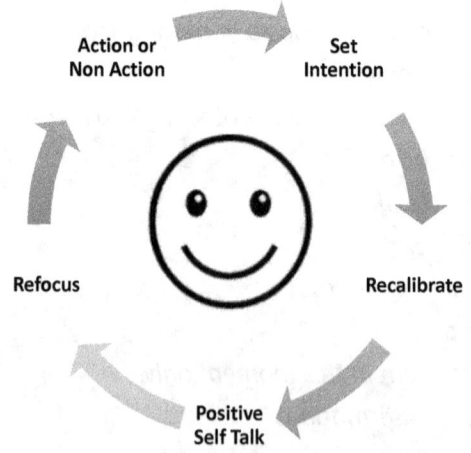

Affirmation and Gratitude

"*As a man thinketh*…so is he"— These words from the Bible (Proverbs 23.7) inspired the title of James Allen's famous 1903 self-help book.

Words have power. What you say to yourself makes an impact on your conscious and unconscious mind. Your words are felt far beyond the person you are talking to. They set up a magnetic energy field that radiates further than you can imagine.

Think of the word "sunshine." What picture did you come up with in your mind? What feeling did it elicit?

Now, think of the word "darkness." What did you notice?

When you say a word, an image is then conjured in your brain. If the image is beautiful, your body and mind respond to this word in a positive way.

If, however, the image is scary, that feeling will be evoked in your body and brain as well.

I still hear my grandmother's words when I called her, and she would say, "It's a beautiful day to be grateful for, the sun is shining, and the birds are singing." My mother's daily affirmation is "I wake in joy, and I sleep in peace" even though she's had many middle of the night calls. However, it helps her immensely when she wakes up throughout the night.

She has her hundreds of self-help books by her side and her meditation tapes which she listens to, and which calm and center her. Whenever she goes somewhere she says, "Expect my Good," and sure enough, a parking spot opens in front of her, no matter how crowded it is. I always try to jinx it because I think the extra walk would do her good; my fitness hat is always on, fortunately or unfortunately for her. My dad has always said "I'm alive, alert and full of enthusiasm" and still does to this day, even as he struggles to walk and see. These positive affirmations have been implanted in my mind so that even when the world around me turns upside down, I have learned not to give power to my negative thoughts.

What words do you use every day? What words do you continue to expose yourself to? If it's the news, you might feel glum all day. How do you protect yourself from these daily bombardments of negativity in advertisements, the newspaper, or people? Bad news spreads faster than good news, and we have become addicted to it. It's how the media survives. Make a point to look for articles that make you smile and lift your spirit.

A thankful and grateful heart creates more abundance and love in your life. It's as simple as that. It's important to affirm what you want every day, and be grateful for what you have done and what you have in your life. This creates a habit of success and self-love, and you automatically start manifesting more abundance in your life. I have a Gratitude Bowl on my desk in my kitchen that I look at every day: I write down something I am grateful for and throw it in the bowl. It doesn't have to be fancy, and you can even write it down in a book, or your journal. The main thing is that you stop to acknowledge what you are grateful for every day. Write down daily at least 6 things for which you are grateful.

Change your words and change your mind

A simple change of saying "I get to teach," rather than, "I must teach" makes a huge shift in how you feel. When I first heard a yoga teacher of mine say it, I realized how different and lighter I felt when I used it in all my daily activities. It is a gift and a privilege to get up in the morning and share what I have learned. What do you get to do? If all you come up with is, "I get to pay my taxes" and sulk about it, think again! At least you can own something, so you can pay taxes.

Words can illuminate your spirit, or kick you to the curb. What are your inner voices doing to you? Start noticing what words you say to yourself, and then ask where they came from. Perhaps they are old tapes you heard growing up.

Let them go. I know, "easier said than done" but do-able. Practice replacing those old tapes with new ones. When we beat ourselves up, we diminish and wilt like a flower without water and sun. When we acknowledge ourselves, we grow and flourish into a beautiful bouquet. Continue to weed the garden of your mind.

Affirmations:

Just for today, I will take each moment and breathe as it comes. I will not judge every little thing I do and berate myself. I will look at the morning dew on the window and notice a bird on the distant horizon. I will be that bird, and fly to new heights, beyond what I thought possible. I will watch the bird until I become one with it, and feel free. And tomorrow I will do it again.

You are enough, and always have been enough. Continue this mantra, and watch life change before your very eyes. Doors will open, and you will see the world from a different vantage point.

It's important you say affirmations or change your self-talk every day.

Example Affirmations:

I am enough.
I am beautiful.
I am learning.
I am loving.
I am wise.
I am strong.
I am deserving.
I am healthy.
I move fluidly.

Your Daily Practice

Having a daily practice to connect you to your spirit is vital for keeping energy flowing through you, so you can access your Higher Power and invite the Divine in to work through you.

Make a list of everything that connects you to your higher self here, and refer back to it often.

My list looks like this:

Stretching either before I get out of bed or right after.
Doing Tai Chi or yoga.
Saying my affirmations, being grateful for another day.
Thanking the divine for the opportunity to serve.
Meditating.
Reading some affirmative books.
Drink warm water with ½ fresh squeezed lemon.
Writing.
Blessing my food and being grateful for food and nourishment.
Walking.
Dancing.
Looking at my garden and appreciating the flowers, birds, squirrels and nature.
Petting and playing with my animals.
Drinking tea or the ritual of staying present to everyday tasks.
Listening to music or a podcast.

It changes from moment to moment as I listen to what is happening inside my body. Expand on what yours is, and make sure you listen to new things that you might not even be in touch with, that you discover feed the deepest part of you.

Ok, it's your turn...

Your Daily Practice

1.
2.
3.
4.
5.
6.
7.

List 7 things every day that you are proud of yourself for!

Examples:

1. *I was on time*
2. *I was kind to myself.*
3. *I meditated.*
4. *I took time to eat slowly and savor each bite.*
5. *I said NO, not at this time.*
6. *I scheduled something I had been putting off.*
7. *I spoke up and told my truth.*

Speaking your truth

While it's not easy to say what's true for you, there was a great price paid for freedom of speech. We are lucky to have voices to use. We can use our voices freely and collectively, to really make a difference in our world.

From a young age, most of us were taught to be respectful and be polite at the expense of how we feel. (I know I was!) No wonder it comes as a surprise when we find that what we really feel compared to what we've been told to feel (reality vs. expectations) is so far off. It can rock our inner world and throw us off balance, leaving us feeling lost and confused. Often, we haven't a clue what we feel, and it takes a long time to break the sheath and peel back the layers to know our truth. We might be so used to squelching all these feelings and thoughts that when they finally come to the surface, it's as though a volcano has erupted, and we feel completely out of control, which can be scary. Only by practice, and taking the time to get used to our authentic self, can liberation and freedom become a celebrated reality.

However, when we stifle our feelings, we close that door to freedom. Inwardly, these emotions set off normal internal responses; some bodily systems, like our immune system, get shut down. As our cortisol levels peak, our bodies are setting off into stress mode. We go into an internal battle, where 'fight or flight' hormones pump through our blood stream.

Our Vishuddha Chakra (energetic system) that is located at our throat, can tighten, resulting in sore throats, tightness, pain, allergies, etc. These emotions: anger, resentment, frustration, and a feeling of suffocation will build up inside when we don't honor our truth and speak it.

Many people don't want to hurt someone's feelings by saying how they really feel, and will endure the suffering internally, often hurting themselves instead by keeping the peace and being quiet. There is no peace in silencing ourselves, but we tell ourselves there is at the expense of our truth. Keeping quiet hurts two people: you and the other person. Your silence does not allow the person to see how their actions and words can affect another person, and you rob them of an opportunity to change and grow, if they so choose. Although there isn't necessarily a right or wrong, it's important to have your voice and communicate what is true for you for optimum health. I can't tell you the amount of people that don't speak up in a bodywork session when the therapist is overstepping a boundary and talking through their session because they don't want to hurt their feelings. I always ask, "wait, who is paying for this session?" The therapist is then using the client to fill their own needs rather than the client's. This is not ok!

Start looking at where you compromise your truth because you don't want to rock the boat or make waves. Maybe the other person has your number and has bullied you enough to shut you up, or you've stooped to their level of screaming and hollering obscenities at each other, to avoid making a necessary change. We get so entangled in either silence or fighting which becomes a vicious cycle where no one wins, and we think this is normal communication. Both set up roadblocks that keep us stuck at an impasse. If you don't want to change, you get to have the same result you always have had, and you know what that is.

On the other hand, if you want a different experience, you must change something to create that. This is your life. What do you want? How do you want to live? I commend you for speaking your truth and having your voice. When we speak our truth, we allow others around us to grow as well. They might not like what you have to say, which is also fine, and they get an opportunity to share their truth with you.

As you do it more, you will get better at it, and it won't be so difficult. In the beginning, it may seem a little harsh because it's so foreign. Be gentle with yourself. It's ok if you don't say it exactly right and someone takes it wrong. As they say, "the truth will set you free." Always remember, life is not stagnant, and we have many opportunities for growth and change. If you don't learn it the first time, you will get another chance, because these lessons keep coming up until we learn them.

Honestly, as I'm writing this, I thought of a little white lie I was about to tell, which gave me another opportunity to walk my talk and be honest. If we never tell a lie, we never have to worry about what to cover up, or say.

In the words of Mahatma Gandhi, *"Silence becomes cowardice when occasion demands speaking out the whole truth and acting accordingly."*

Some Closing Thoughts

What is life if we come to the end with questions still unanswered? And yet, what is life without query?

We glorify our past, or mourn our choices.

Hard and rigid bodies reflect closed mind thinking.

Regret can be sobering, yet useless, unless we can rectify what's been done.

Looking back and reliving happy moments brings us comfort and joy, yet be forewarned of becoming stuck in the past.

Staying present to what is can be hard work, when loss around you is so great that pain replaces pleasure.

Our breath and affirmations sustain us and set us free: but making use of them is easier said than done, so practice daily.

Take each moment as it comes, and stay in the now as much as possible.

Peace is a state of mind.

Acceptance is the cornerstone of contentment.

*Torrential downpour
floodgates burst enabling
healing waters flow*

Afterward: Celebrate!

So…. You've made it through the book, Congratulations!

Who are you NOW? Take a minute to answer that question and see what's changed.

Cheers and congratulations, on reading and hopefully doing a lot of the workbook pages as well. It's been my honor to share my journey with you in creating the life you are born to have. I can't wait to hear your wins and successes. You can always come back to these questions and do them over from time to time. Use it as a go-to book when you are setting out on a new intention and setting another objective. These tried-and-true methods work, and the degree to which you are honest and take the time to cement them, is the degree to which you will benefit from them.

Life is meant to be celebrated at every stage of the journey. As much as I balk at Hallmark moments, because they feel like so much hype and commercialism, I still view them as an opportunity to come together, pause and pay homage to those we love.

We need to celebrate each moment, and take each lesson as it comes up, which sometimes means crying through the tears until they pass, and laughing through the ridiculous. Finding laughter through obstacles is so vital, and there is nothing like a good ole belly laugh to remind you not to take life too seriously. Life continues to bless us daily with gifts and opportunities, and it is here that we find nuggets of inspiration and pearls of wisdom to carry us through in joy and love.

As we come to a close, I am hopeful that our journey together here on the page will inspire you to reach your full potential, and continue to help you grow as a person, each and every day.

Remember to brush yourself off when you fall down or have a setback and rise back taller than before.

Acknowledge your small wins as well as your big ones daily, and be grateful for each day. It is in this practice that we Re-Create our lives and *Celebrate* the abundance that is rightfully ours. Remember your daily affirmations, and make peace with silence. It is here that you create your reality. I am here to cheer you on and remind you of your greatness and how deserving you are.

Acknowledgements

First and foremost, I want to thank my parents for bringing me into this world and the many lessons and blessings they have given me. My mother thanks me often for coming through her to teach her so much about living life and growth, and I am astonished to watch her continue to blossom in the world, giving her gifts though healing touch. She has always been my biggest cheerleader. Thank you beyond words for your love and support through every moment of my journey, and for being here for our 4 kids. My dad often says, "I wish I would have seen you more when you were growing up, gone to your games and activities," and just hearing him say that means the world to me. I love you, Dad! Going back and healing the mother / father wound is a gift, whether your parents are alive or not, but truly life altering to do, no matter what.

To my brother and his family: My love and prayers are always with you. To my niece Misty, I'm so proud of you for making your way as an independent competent young woman. Congratulations!

To my husband, who truly is the wind beneath my sails, no matter if we don't always see eye to eye on, well, almost anything. Haha! I deeply love you beyond words, and you more than made up for all the wounds of my past, and have always seen me. I am so appreciative of your love and support, and thank you from the bottom of my heart, while I healed my past trauma and found myself. I know I give you a run for your money, and I am astonished by your steadfast love and the amazing father you are to our children and soon-to-be grandchildren.

To my friends and clients who are the cornerstone of my day and feed me spiritually and emotionally. I am so blessed to know you. The gifts you bring by your love, courage, strength, belly laughs, honesty and faith truly inspire me to be the best I can be in life. I learn from you daily. Thank you for your friendship and mutual admiration. There are too many to mention here. I love you all.

To my kids who are my heart and soul. I can't tell you how much I love you and how proud of each one of you I am. Each of you radiate so much love and so are similar and yet so different in your own authentic way. I'm so grateful to be your mom and watch you mark the world with your magic and authenticity.

To Dr. Cherie Carter Scott for being a mentor and training me to be a life coach and supporting me in my journey as a Fitness Health coach. I am so honored to know you for 40 plus years and your constant wisdom in each endeavor, and it's an honor to have you as a mentor, colleague and friend. I am so grateful to you for writing the foreword to my book. In deepest gratitude.

To Bonnie Sabrina McGuire for supporting me through the

trauma of my fears and worries, reassuring me that I wasn't crazy and the only thing that was wrong with me was thinking I was. I can't thank you enough for helping me identify and make friends with the many voices, and accept their guidance as warning signs to take care of me on the deepest level. I am forever grateful.

To my town that holds me together after 45 years as a community in business, friendship and comradery. There is something about a small town that is so rewarding and rich, and I feel so lucky to have so many acquaintances and deep friendships with so many of you.

To my blog family who sees me more than anyone else does these days and shows up to support my writing no matter what I write and has so much insight, wisdom, and positivity even when I think I missed the mark. Thank you truly and to all of you who have been so kind to offer to review my book and support me, which I am beyond grateful for.

A special thanks to Yvette from Priorhouse blog who has been a fan of my poetry and given me so much guidance and support, always cheering me on and offering to help me.

To Gabriela Maria Milton for her mentorship in writing, inviting me to be a contributing author for MasticadoresUSA for the last year and counting, being a contributing author in 2 of her best-selling anthologies, *Wounds I Healed* and *Hidden in Childhood*. Your gifts in poetry are extraordinary. I am so very appreciative of your review of my book which I cherish and value, thank you.

To Ingrid Wilson from Experiments in Fiction for being an extraordinary editor, stretching me and believing in my book and workbook. She personally went through it, not only as an editor, but also as a participant and gave me a thumbs up and the encouragement I needed to get my book into the world. She said, "It's a great book and people need to hear your message."

Her professionalism, insights, friendship, and chats have truly been a Godsend and seen this book to fruition. Thank you so much!

And finally, to my animals who love me no matter what, and keep me in bed longer than I should at times, but their snuggles and love are my world.

— Cindy Georgakas, March 2023

Also Available From EIF

The Colourblind Grief
by Jude Gorini

ISBN: 9781739404406

London 2011, the year before the Olympics. The city is buzzing, and Daniel is just starting his journey into self-destruction: living a life of toxic love as his only remaining option. Sex, drugs and rock & roll are his sustenance. His mental health issues warp his life. 10 years later, everything has changed. Was it just a lie created by his family, or by his mind?

A rip-roaring ride of a confessional novel, which takes place within the gay club scene of East London, before moving to Europe and the serene, sandy beaches of La Graciosa. Jude Gorini has written a brave, uncompromising tale which deals with issues of mental health, sexual identity and self-discovery. Difficult to put down, and impossible to forget!

Archery in the UK
by Nick Reeves and Ingrid Wilson

ISBN: 9781739757786

Inspired by the *Lyrical Ballads* of Wordsworth and Coleridge, two authors set out to pen a contemporary homage to this timeless collection. As the collaboration progresses, however, the poetry and the unique narrative it carries takes on a life of its own. Thus, the authors come to tell their story through a collection of ballads, sonnets, pantoums and other forms: under arches, over bridges and against the backdrop of the fabled Northlands: from Tyne and Wear to Cumbria and beyond.

40 Poems At 40
by Ingrid Wilson

ISBN: 9781739757700

40 Poems is the debut poetry collection from Ingrid Wilson. It is poetry of place and space, and here lie the clues and the beauty to Wilson's poetry. Her work is charted, landscaped, travelled, explorative and laden with adventure. There are bright, sad, dreamy postcards telling of the beauty of Barcelona, the slate-grey, but singing, county of Cumbria, Malaga, 'the emptiness' of Manchester, 'the fields' of London, 'the ancient pasts' of Newcastle, the mysterious beauty of Slovenia, Venice and its lullaby… lapping water is never far from her ear.

A reflective, rich debut that reveals, in startling images and with dextrous word-play, a trove for those of us learning to live and to love.

***Wounds I Healed: The Poetry of Strong Women*
edited by Gabriela Marie Milton**

ISBN: 9781739757724

Award-winning authors, Pushcart nominees, emerging poets, voices of women and men, come to the fore in this stunning, powerful, and unique anthology. These poems testify both to the challenges that women face in our society, and to their power to overcome them. A memorable collection of over 200 poems by more than 100 authors, this anthology is a must-have for all lovers of poetry. We all can benefit from the poetry of survival, and of healing. We all can benefit from the experiences so beautifully evoked in this book. We can all come together to emerge triumphant from pain.

***Nature Speaks of Love and Sorrow*
by Jeff Flesch**

ISBN: 9781739757755

In this hotly-anticipated debut poetry collection from Jeff Flesch, the author invites us to take a voyage with him through trauma and pain into acceptance and bliss in the embrace of nature itself. Jeff's poems are infused with the textures and colours of the natural world, and his journey through this sensory paradise provides the backdrop to his inner journey towards healing and growth.

***Three-Penny Memories, A Poetic Memoir*
by Barbara Harris Leonhard**

ISBN: 9781739757762

"Do you love your mother?"

— This provocative question provides the catalyst for this stunning poetic memoir from Barbara Harris Leonhard. Through her artfully crafted poetry, the author considers where her love and loyalties lie following her aging mother's diagnosis with Alzheimer's.

www.ingramcontent.com/pod-product-compliance
Lightning Source LLC
Chambersburg PA
CBHW071348080526
44587CB00017B/3018